SAMSUNG GALAX USER MANUA EXPERIENCE

Discover the splendors of the latest S series super smartphone

Timothy Dan

Table of Contents

INTRODUCTION

The new Snapdragon 8 Gen 3 is intended to be used by the Samsung Galaxy S24 Ultra everywhere in the world. It has 256GB, 512GB, or 1TB of UFS 4.0 storage together with 12GB of LPDDR5X RAM.

Better thermal performance is expected since Samsung increased the vapor chamber from the Galaxy S23 Ultra by almost twofold.

Samsung's "smartest AI phone ever" is the Galaxy S24 Ultra, thanks to the Snapdragon 8 Gen 3 processor. With the phone's on-demand Live Translate feature, you may talk in other languages directly within the app and have real-time translations provided. As part of One UI 6.1, further AI features will include a Smart Keyboard and Dynamic Lock Screen.

The S Pen is a standout feature of the Galaxy S Ultra, and the S24 Ultra also contains one.

Samsung has upgraded its camera with a new 5x camera module, which is probably going to be a 50MP periscope device. That translates to about 120mm in terms of optical length, and by using its superior sensor and optics to the current 10x camera, it will also function as a 10x and 100x shooter.

Regarding video, the primary camera can record in 8K at up to 30 frames per second and in 4K at up to 120 frames per second.

The 5,000mAh battery of the Galaxy S24 Ultra is identical to that of its predecessors, with the same 45W wired and 15W wireless charging capabilities as well as a 30-minute charging time of 0-65%.

The Samsung Galaxy S24 Ultra has emergency messaging via satellite support via the 3GPP standard out of the box, however it's unclear if this functionality will be available in other areas and how much it will cost.

Although the camera's optical hardware remains same (5x), a number of enhancements have been implemented with the new chipset.

The main camera images on the Galaxy S24 Ultra have been AI-optimized. Samsung apparently made sure to use a new algorithm that recognizes 12 different types of objects to correct the Galaxy S23 Ultra's murky output.

The best mode is night mode. Photos taken at night with the zoom cameras are brighter thanks to Nightography Zoom. Another AI function is called Generative Edit, which allows you to rearrange objects, delete them, or replace a space with anything you wish (a Samsung account and an Internet connection are needed for this).

Galaxy S24 Ultra

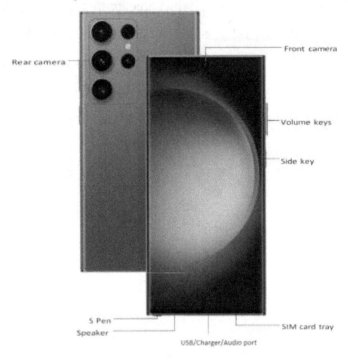

Rear camera

Front camera

Volume keys

Side key

S Pen

Speaker

USB/Charger/Audio port

SIM card tray

Galaxy S24+

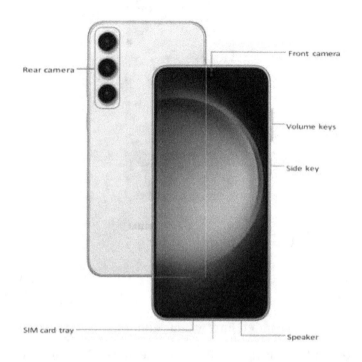

Front camera

Rear camera

Volume keys

Side key

SIM card tray

Speaker

Nano-SIM cards are used in your device. You can either use your old card or the device may have a pre-installed SIM. The 5G network indicators are based on the availability of the network and the specifications of your service provider.

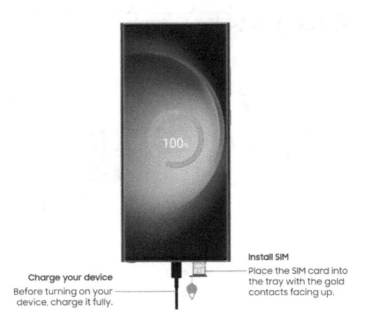

Charge your device
Before turning on your
device, charge it fully.

Install SIM
Place the SIM card into
the tray with the gold
contacts facing up.

The Samsung Galaxy S24+ is IP68 certified, which means it can endure water and dust. To ensure its durability, make sure that your device's SIM card tray is always free of dust. Securely inserting the tray into the device before being exposed to liquids is also important.

Maintaining water and dust resistance

Never charge your device while it's wet to avoid getting damaged or electric shock. Also, avoid using the device or charging cords with wet hands.

The Galaxy S24+ is not designed to withstand water and dust damage. It should be closed tightly in order to prevent it from getting damaged.

Follow these tips to keep your device protected and its water and dust resistance functions running smoothly.

IP68 certification means that the Galaxy S24+ can endure water and dust. This ensures that it can withstand submersion in fresh water.

Keep the device submerged for at least 30 minutes to ensure that it doesn't get damaged. After washing it, use a soft cloth to thoroughly clean it. If you're worried that your device might get damaged after being exposed to non-water, submerge it in fresh water for a couple of minutes.

All devices with ports and compartments that can be accessed should have these closed tightly so that liquid cannot enter the system.

If the device has been submerged in water or the speaker of the device has been wet, it may not be able to provide the best sound quality during a call. To prevent this issue, always wipe the device with a dry rag before using it.

The water and dust resistance features of the device may get damaged if it is dropped or gets hit. Foreign objects or dust may also enter the receiver, speaker, or microphone.

Some of the device's functions may not work or sound may become quieter. If a sharp object is used to remove dust or foreign materials, it may damage the device and its appearance.

An air vent hole may become covered by an accessory, which could cause unwanted noises to emerge during media playback or calls.

The presence of liquid other than fresh water can speed up the entry of fluids into the device. Failure to thoroughly clean and rinse the device may result in cosmetic or operability issues.

CHAPTER ONE

Charge the battery

A rechargeable battery powers up your device.

Always use the Samsung-approved charging cables and chargers for your device. In order to prevent damage or injury, avoid using devices with mismatched or worn batteries or other incompatible accessories. Also, using other devices that have not been certified by Samsung may lead to issues.

When the charging cable and the device become too hot, it may prevent the device from fully charging. This issue usually doesn't affect the device's performance or lifespan. If this occurs, you can try unplugging the charger and waiting for the device to cool itself down. You can also contact Samsung's support team through its website at support@samsung.com.

Wireless power sharing

Using your phone to power up compatible Samsung devices is not supported while using wireless power.

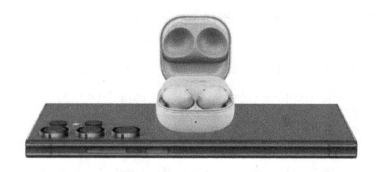

In the Device Settings app, go to the Battery option and choose Wireless power sharing.

Select the percentage of battery capacity that you want to use. When the device reaches this level of charging, the wireless power sharing feature will automatically stop.

Go to the Settings app and select the "Power Sharing" option.

When placing the device on the back to charge, a vibration or notification sound may occur as the charging begins.

Most Qi-compliant devices work seamlessly with wireless power sharing. The speed and efficiency of the charge vary depending on the device. Some models may not work with certain covers or accessories, and you should remove them if you experience slow or problematic charging.

Please note that the wireless power sharing feature is best used with devices that comply with Qi.

Before you start using the wireless power sharing feature, make sure that you have removed any accessories that are not compatible with the device.

The placement of the charging coil may vary for different devices. In order to make a connection, you'll need to adjust this part of the setup. Once the charging session has started, a vibration or notification will appear, letting you know that you have made a connection.

Data and call services may experience an impact, depending on your region's network environment. Also, the efficiency and speed of the wireless power sharing may vary. You should refrain from using headphones while using the feature.

Turn on your device.

The Side key should be used to turn on your device. Don't use it if the device is broken or cracked, and only use it after it has been fixed.

To turn it on, press and hold the Side key.

To turn off your device, hold the Volume down and Side keys simultaneously. Then, press and hold the Power off button. You'll be prompted to confirm.

Restart your device by holding both the Volume down and Side keys at the same time. You'll be asked to confirm.

To learn more about powering your device on and off, go to the Advanced features section and select the Side key option.

The optimal 5G experience requires a fast and unobstructed connection with an antenna positioned correctly on the rear of the device. In addition, 5G may be affected by a cover or case.

Use the Setup Wizard

The first time you turn on your device, the wizard will guide you through the steps in setting up your device.

You'll be prompted to follow the steps to configure your device and connect to a Wi-Fi network. You can also set up accounts, locate services, and learn more about its features.

Bring data from an old device

You can easily transfer photos, music, messages, notes, calendar entries, and contacts from your old device with the help of Smart Switch. It can be done through a computer, a USB cable, or Wi-Fi.

To learn more about the features of Smart Switch, please visit the company's website at samsung.com/smartswitch.

After navigating to the settings, select the option to bring data from your old device and follow the prompts.

The lock screen and security features are available on your device. They can be used to protect your device whenever the screen is not active. More information about these features can be found in the app or in the security section.

The images presented are for illustrative purposes only and do not reflect the current state of the art of software and devices.

Side key settings

The shortcuts that are assigned to the Side key can be customized. You can also choose which features are launched whenever the Side key is pressed multiple times.

Side key
Press to lock.
Press to turn on the screen, and then swipe the screen to unlock it.

To enable the quick launch camera, double-press the + symbol. You'll be asked to choose an option that says "Open app" or "Quick launch camera."

Press and hold

You can choose which features are launched whenever the Side key is pressed multiple times. From the Settings app, go to the Advanced features section and select

30

the Side key option. You can also set up accounts and manage your contacts, email, and calendar.

Add a Google Account

To access your Google Cloud storage and other installed apps, sign in to your Google Account. You can also use the device's various Android features.

After you've set up a lock screen and signed in to a Google account, Google Device Protection will automatically activate. This feature requires your Google account details when you reset to factory settings.

Go to the Settings app and select the option to manage your contacts, backup, and accounts. You can also add a Samsung account to your Google account.

Add a Samsung account

Sign in using your Samsung account to gain access to exclusive content and utilize Samsung apps.

You can add a Samsung account and sign in using Outlook to view and manage your messages. From the settings, 🅒 go to the Manage accounts and backup section, then select the option to add an account.

First-time users can set up their voicemail 📼 feature. The options for different service providers may vary. You can also access voicemail with the Phone app.

Hold the 1 key and tap Voicemail. 📼 Follow the instructions to create a password and record a greeting, as well as your name.

CHAPTER TWO

Navigation

The best way to use a touch screen is with a light touch using a finger or a stylus.

Tap

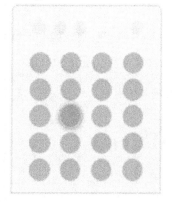

However, excessive force or the use of a metallic object on the screen may damage it. This issue won't be covered by the device's warranty.

Swipe

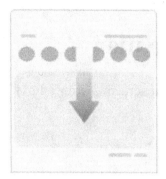

You can drag and drop an item to its new location or add a shortcut to it to the Home screen. You can also move it to a different area by dragging a widget.

Drag and drop

You can zoom in and out of the screen using your thumb or finger.

To zoom in, move your thumb and index finger apart. Then, move your thumb and index finger together to zoom out.

To activate certain features, touch or hold an item.

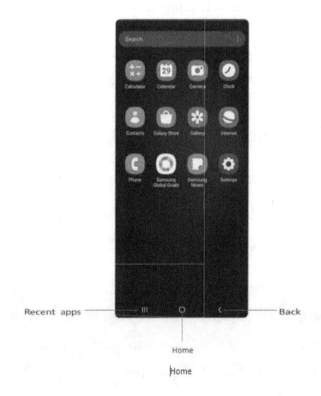

Recent apps

Back

Home

Home

Hold the field to show the pop-up menu or touch the Home screen to customize it.

Navigation bar

You can use gestures or the navigation buttons to navigate the device. The home button is located at the bottom of the screen, and it allows users to quickly access the various features of the device.

Under the Button order, choose which part of the Home screen the recent apps and Back icons will appear on.

Navigation gestures

To get an unobstructed view of the device, remove the navigation buttons from the bottom of the screen. Instead, swipe to navigate through it.

Go to the Settings app and choose the option to enable the gesture recognition feature. You can also customize it by choosing a sensitivity or gesture type. The gesture hints appear at the bottom of the screen.

You can still switch apps using gestures even if gesture hint is disabled. You can also hide the keyboard by showing an icon at the bottom right corner. This feature works when the device is being used in portrait mode.

You can prevent the S Pen from using navigation gestures by blocking gestures. This works on the Galaxy S23 Ultra only.

Customize your home screen

The Home screen is the primary place where you can navigate your device. You can customize it by adding new ones, removing them, and setting the order of the various screens.

The Home screen can serve as the launchpad for an app if you want to use it. You can add an app by holding and touching its icon, or you can remove it by holding and touching its icon. Keep in mind that taking an icon from the Home screen does not remove the app.

You can change the look of the Lock and Home screens by choosing a specific image or video or a preloaded wallpaper.

Hold and touch the Home screen to access the style and Wallpaper options. You can then tap on the images and the Lock screen to change them. You can also download and install various wallpapers from the Galaxy Themes app.

You can select a color palette based on the colors of your wallpaper. You can also enable the dimming option for your wallpaper when the Dark mode is turned on. You can then set a theme that will be applied to the home and lock screens, app icons, and wallpapers.

To download and install themes, go to the Themes app and choose the one that you want. Then, tap on the "Apply" button to apply it. You can also replace the default icons with different ones. To preview and download the selected icons, go to the Themes app and tap on the "icons" option.

Go to the My stuff > Icons section and choose the icon set that you want to apply. After selecting the set, tap on the icon to apply it. Widgets allow you to easily access various apps and information on your home screens.

Go to the home screen and swipe to the widget that you want to add. You can then customize its appearance and function by pressing the "Add" button. You can also create a stack of similar sized items to make them appear in the same place.

You can remove a widget from your home screen. You can also customize its appearance and function by going to the settings. In the app info section, you can review the permissions, usage, and more of the widget.

You can customize the layout of your home screen by setting it to have separate home and apps screens. You can also only have one home screen where all of your apps are located.

The grid layout for the home screen will determine how the icons are displayed. The grid for the apps will show you the arrangement of the icons. The layout for folders will also be used to determine how they are organized.

You can add a media page to the home screen by swiping right from the area that you want to view it. You can then tap the available services to view their content.

You can show the apps screen with a button on the home screen. This lets you easily access the various apps that are currently running.

Items within the home screen may not be moved or removed.

Items within the home screen can be locked and prevented from being moved or removed. You can also automatically add new apps to the home screen.

To hide apps from the home and apps screens, select the ones that you want to hide. You can then return to this screen to retrieve the hidden apps. These are still installed and can be found in the Finder searches.

Enable the ability to show app icon badges with notifications active. You can select the style of badge that you want to use.

You can enable the ability to swipe down to open the notification panel using anywhere on the home screen.

When your device's orientation changes from portrait to landscape mode, the home screen will automatically rotate once more.

The home screen of your device has a variety of information and options. You can also contact Samsung through its support channel.

Easy mode

The Easy mode layout utilizes larger icons and text for a more organized and visually appealing experience. You can switch between the default and simpler layouts when needed.

To enable this feature, go to the home screen and tap on the option that you want to enable.

One of the options that you can enable is the delay in the recognition of touch and hold. This allows you to set the time it takes for the continuous touch to be considered a hold and touch.

You can select a keyboard with vibrant colors by going to the settings and choosing High contrast.

Apps list

The products and software of Samsung are constantly evolving, so the illustrations presented here are for reference only.

Status bar

The status bar provides various information about the device, such as its battery level and location. It also displays notifications on the left side. Some of these include a call in progress, an alarm, and a new message.

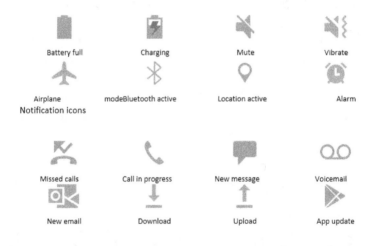

To configure the status bar for notifications, go to the Quick settings and select More options.

Notification panel

The Notification panel is accessible from any screen. It gives you quick access to settings, notifications, and more. You can swipe down to the notification panel and open an item. Alternatively, you can drag the notification to the right or left side to remove it.

These illustrations are only meant to be used as a reference. The software and devices of Samsung are constantly changing, so these are not the same as the ones shown here.

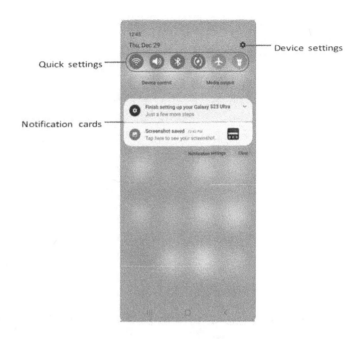

Quick settings

Device settings

Notification cards

Go to the settings and select Clear all notifications. You can also customize the notifications by going to the Customize option and selecting the desired style. Drag the notification from the bottom right corner upward or down to close the notification panel.

The Quick settings provide quick access to various functions through the Notification panel. The icons shown below show the most frequently used settings in

Quick settings. Other options may be found on your device.

Drag the notification bar down to reveal the panel. From the top of the screen, swipe down again to reveal the Quick settings. You can also tap on a quick icon to activate or deactivate it. Release the icon and hold it to open the settings. Wi-Fi Sound, Bluetooth Auto rotate, Location Power saving Dark mode, and others are available.

To find your device, go to the device's search bar, scroll down, and click on the Power off and Restart option. Navigate to the device's settings, and change the layout of the button or the Quick settings.

Enabled apps, such as Google Home and SmartThings, will let you control other devices.

The Media output feature allows users to control the playback of content from their connected devices.

The Media output feature lets users control the playback of content from their connected devices. It also provides a slider that allows users to adjust the brightness.

CHAPTER THREE

S Pen

The S Pen has a variety of useful features, such as launching apps, taking notes, and drawing pictures. Some of these may not work if your device is located near a magnet.

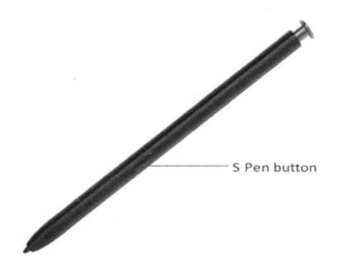

S Pen button

Remove the S Pen

The S Pen can be found in the bottom of your device, and it charges to allow users to use it remotely.

To remove the S Pen, press the stylus inward and slide it out.

To ensure that your device's water-resistant features are protected, make sure that the opening and slot for the S Pen are clean and free of dust and water. The stylus should also be securely inserted before being exposed to liquids.

The images presented here are for illustrative purposes only and do not reflect the current state of software and devices.

Air view

The Air view mode allows users to hover the S Pen over their device's screen to take a quick look at content or find information about an item.

Prior to opening an email message, users can preview it, as well as the contents of an album or a picture. They can also examine a video or navigate to a particular scene by hovering over it. The ability to preview content is only available if the on-screen pointer of the S Pen is in a solid color.

Air Actions

With the S Pen, users can perform remote tasks using their gestures or button. They can set their own shortcuts for their favorite apps, navigate their devices, and complete their actions.

Only Samsung-approved S Pen devices with BLE support can use the remote feature. If the stylus is too far away, it will disconnect from the device. Users must also connect the device to use Air actions.

To enable the Air actions feature, go to the Settings app and select Advanced features. Then, hold the button shortcut for the S Pen.

Hold the S Pen button shortcut

When holding the S Pen button, users can set a shortcut for the camera app. This shortcut is typically set to launch the app.

To enable the Air actions feature, go to the Settings app and select Advanced features. Then, hold the Pen button and press the "Air actions" button.

Using the stylus while performing different gestures, such as up, down, right, or shake, users can access anywhere actions, which can be accessed from any aspect of their device. These shortcuts can be used with apps, navigation, and various other features.

Go to Settings, select Advanced features, and then choose Air actions. In the next section, go to the Gesture icon, and then select the option for "Customize." You can also use the stylus to perform specific actions within specific apps.

Back		Left to right
Recents		Right to left
Home		Up and down
Smart select		Down and up
Screen write		Zigzag

General app actions

To navigate through the various shortcuts, go to the Settings app and select Advanced features. Then, look for the shortcuts that you want to enable.

While using media and camera apps that aren't in the app action list, you can customize the general actions of those apps.

Tap the Advanced features option under the Air actions and S Pen categories. Under the general app actions section, tap on the option to change it.

Screen off memo

You can write memos on the device without turning it on. To do so, you must enable the screen-off mode.

After enabling screen-off mode, remove the S Pen and write on the device's screen. You can also customize the color of the pen and its settings. You can also use a pen tool to change the thickness of the line, and you can use the eraser tool to wipe all of your memos. You can save your notes to the S Pen app.

When the S Pen has been removed from the device and the screen is off, press the button and tap it to start writing notes.

Pin to Always On Display

You can pin or change a memo on the Always On display. To do so, tap on the screen off memo and then tap on the Pin to Always On feature.

Air command

Sign in with the signature features of the S Pen, such as Screen write, Smart select, and Samsung Notes, on any screen.

To use the Air command, ⬤✎ hold the S Pen at the screen and then press the button once.

To create a new note, tap on the option to launch it in the ⊕ Samsung Notes app. You can also view all of your ▤ notes by launching the app and viewing a listing of the notes that you made.

All of the illustrations presented are for reference only and are not indicative of the actual conditions of your device or software.

Samsung Notes has various features that allow you   to create and collect various types of illustrations. You can also doodle using the AR camera. You can create animated messages and live drawings using the S Pen.

Hover the S Pen over a certain word and it will translate it into another language. You can also listen to its pronunciation.

You can use the S Pen to create and share live illustrations, as well as color and edit them. You can also add more apps and functions to the Air menu through the Add button.

You can customize the Air command by adding more functions and apps to the menu or changing the way it appears.

Create note

Launch a new note within the app of Samsung Notes and then view all of your notes. You can also launch the app and view a listing of all of the notes that you created. Tap the Air command to view all of your notes.

Smart select

The Smart select feature is useful if you want to copy and paste content from one screen to another. It can be used to add it to your gallery app or share it across your contacts.

To use the Smart select feature, tap on the option to launch the app and then view all of your notes. There are various options that you can choose from, such as Pin/Insert, which allows you to add a shortcut to the content that you want to extract. Auto select is also useful if you want to automatically select the content that you want to extract.

You can draw on the content that has been captured, identify and extract the text, or choose to share it.

Tap the Animation option to create and pin an animated image or video to the screen using Smart select.

Screen write

You can capture screenshots and draw on them using the Screen write feature. You can start by pressing the Air command and then tap on the option to capture the current screen. You can then use the pen tool to edit the captured content.

To customize the size, color, and tip of the pen, tap the icon twice.

The eraser will remove the drawings or writing ⬤ on the screenshot. Undoing will undo the last action. Sharing will let you share the content. Scroll capture will take care of hiding areas on the screen. The content will be saved to the Gallery app.

The eraser will remove all writing and drawings from the screenshot. Undoing allows you to reverse the last action. Redo the last one to repeat it. Sharing lets you distribute your content. Scroll capture will remove any areas of the screen that are not visible. The content will then be saved to the app Gallery.

To remove drawings from the screen, hold the S Pen button. You can also use the Live messages feature to record an animated message or a written one. To choose the background option, go to Air > Live messages.

You can view all of the live messages that you've created and choose the background image that you want. You can also capture an image to use as the background.

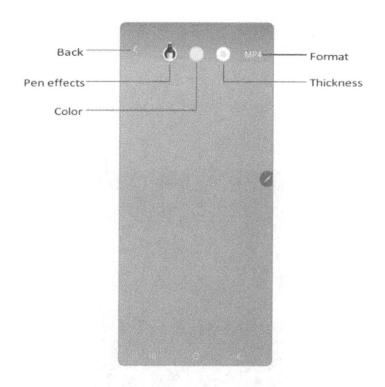

Back ——— Format

Pen effects ——— Thickness

Color

Pick the color that you want for the background. Follow the prompts to start recording your live message, and then tap Done to save.

The illustrations shown here are only for reference purposes. The devices and software used are constantly evolving.

AR Doodle

You can doodle on different faces or objects that are captured using the camera with augmented reality.

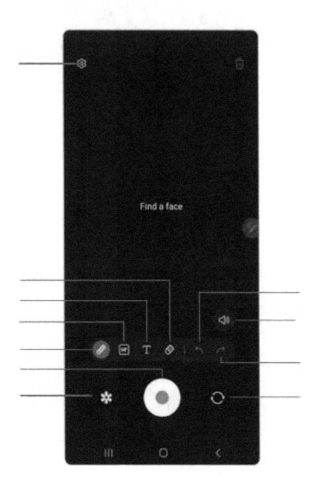

You can start by going to Air > AR Doodle and choosing the option to tap on the front or rear cameras . Switch the cameras to position your target in the middle of the screen. Lastly, use the S Pen to create a doodle.

The doodle follows the face's movements in real-time. You can also save a video of it by pressing Record.

The software and devices used are constantly evolving, so the illustrations presented here are only for reference.

With the S Pen, you can translate words and hear their pronunciation using the app. You can go to Air > Translation and choose the option to switch between translating words and phrases. You can also change the target and source languages by pressing the respective button.

Hover the S Pen over a certain word and then tap Sound to hear its pronunciation in the language of the source. You can also copy and paste the translated text to your clipboard. Finally, close Translate by pressing the Close button.

You can customize the Air menu by adding shortcuts for various apps and functions. To do so, go to Air ⬤ > Add and choose the apps or functions that you want to add. ⊕ To remove a shortcut, tap the "remove" button. You can then save your selection by going to the "Save" section.

To add shortcuts to the Air menu, go to Air > Preferences > Add and choose the app or function that you want to be added. You can then ▬ remove or add these shortcuts by pressing the "remove" option. To save your selection, tap the "Save" section at the bottom.

Air Command settings

The Air menu provides a convenient and collapsible way to access various apps and features, as well as the S Pen.

The Air menu is designed to provide a collapsible and convenient way to access various apps and features, as well as the S Pen.

To configure the Air menu, go to Settings and select Advanced features. Then, choose the menu style that you want to use for the menu.

The Air command has a variety of shortcuts that you can choose from, and you can additionally show or hide an icon for the menu.

The Air command can be opened using the pen button. The settings for the S Pen can be customized. Depending on the service provider, the options for the stylus may be changed.

Go to the Advanced features section and select the S Pen option. Then, configure the Air actions to allow you to control your device while using apps.

The Air command lets you customize the menu's behavior, appearance, and shortcuts. The Air view, on the other hand, can be turned off or on.

S Pen users can write in various text areas such as search fields and address bars with the stylus. It converts handwriting into text and allows users to edit it.

When the S Pen is removed, users can select what happens when they detach it. They can open the Air command, create a note, or do nothing.

When the screen is turned off, users can detach the S Pen and write using it on the screen. They can then save their screen off memos in Samsung Notes.

Hold the S Pen button and then tap the screen multiple times to prompt a new note.

You can configure the various behaviors of the S Pen, such as vibrations and connections.

The latest version of the S Pen is shown here, as well as information about its features. You can also contact Samsung through its members.

Bixby

Samsung's virtual assistant, Bixby, is capable of learning and adapting to its users. It can help 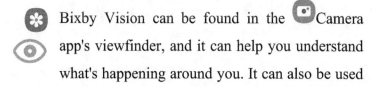 set reminders based on your location and time, and it can also be used in your favorite apps.

To access Bixby, go to your home screen and press and hold the side key. You can also access it through the apps list.

Bixby Vision

With Bixby, you'll have a better understanding of what you're looking at as it works with your Gallery, Internet, and Camera apps. It also has icons for shopping, translating, and QR code detection.

Camera

Bixby Vision can be found in the Camera app's viewfinder, and it can help you understand what's happening around you. It can also be used on photos and images that have been saved in the Gallery app.

In the Internet ⬤ app, you can use Bixby Vision to search for information about an image that you've found there. You can also follow the prompts to access the settings and perform various tasks.

Modes and Routines

You can configure routines and modes to help your device change its ⬤settings automatically based on your specific situation or activity.

To configure your device, go to the Settings app and click on the "Modes" and "Routines" sections. You can select a mode based on your location or activities. You can also create routines for your phone based on your time and surroundings.

Digital wellbeing and parental controls

You can monitor your digital activities by keeping track of how often you open apps, receive notifications, and check your device. You may also set your device to wake you up before sleeping.

Go to the Settings app and click on the Digital Wellbeing and Parental Controls sections. You'll be able to view the various features of this app by scrolling through the dashboard. Here, you can see how long an app has been used and opened, as well as the number of notifications that have been sent out daily.

You can set a goal for your screen time and see your daily average. You can also set a limit on how long an app can be used.

The driving monitor will help you keep track of how much time you spend on your screen and which apps you prefer to use.

A sound source can be used to determine the volume and ensure your ears are protected.

Google's Family Link app is a parental control tool that lets you supervise the digital life of your kids. You can set specific content filters, limit the time spent on screen, and choose apps.

Always On Display

You can view missed calls and messages, as well as check the time and date of your appointments, using Always On Display.

To enable the feature, go to the settings and click on the Always On Display option. You can then configure the timing of when notifications and a clock will appear on the device's screen when it's not in use.

You can change the look of the clock face and the color options for Always On Display and the lock screen.

The music details of the playlist will be shown to you whenever the FaceWidgets Music Controller is enabled. The AOD can also be displayed in landscape or portrait orientation. You can also change the brightness automatically with the help of the software update.

You can easily download and install custom themes for your device using the Always On Display feature. To do so, go to your home screen and tap on the 🪣 "Themes" category. You can then preview and download the files to your device. You can also use biometric security to log in to your accounts and secure your device.

You can use facial recognition to access your device's screen. To use this feature, you must first set a password, PIN, or pattern.

CHAPTER FOUR

Face recognition

Some facial recognition features may be affected by certain factors, such as makeup, facial hair, and glasses.

Make sure that the camera lens is clean and well-lit when you're preparing to register your face. You can follow the prompts to complete the process and set up facial recognition.

An alternative appearance can also be used to enhance the facial recognition feature.

You can enable or disable facial recognition security.

When you enable facial recognition and use it to unlock your device, you should always stay on the lock screen while swiping the screen.

When using facial recognition, it only recognizes your face if you are open.

To make sure that facial recognition can recognize your face in low light conditions, try increasing the brightness of your device.

Learn more about how to use facial recognition to safeguard your device.

Fingerprint scanner

For additional security, you can use a fingerprint scanner instead of typing passwords in some applications.

In order to verify your identity, you can use your fingerprint to access your Samsung account. Before you can use your fingerprint to log in, you must first create a password, PIN or pattern.

Go to the Settings app and select "Security and privacy" and "Biometrics." Then, follow the prompts to enter your fingerprint. You can also delete, rename, or add fingerprints.

Fingerprint management

The list of fingerprints is the top one. You can rename or remove it by tapping on it.

You can add or remove fingerprints. You can also check whether your fingerprint has been registered by scanning it. You can use fingerprint authentication to access your device's apps and perform other actions to verify your identity. To set up this feature, go to the settings app and select "Biometrics" and "security and privacy."

Use your fingerprint to unlock your device. You can also use it to check whether your fingerprint is registered by scanning it, regardless of the screen being off. You can also show an animation when you're using fingerprint verification.

You should know more about how to protect your device using fingerprints. You can configure your biometric security preferences in the settings app.

The transition effect will show whenever you use biometric authentication to unlock your device.

In this article, we'll talk about how to use biometrics to secure your device.

Multi window

You can multitask by using several applications at the same time. With Multi window technology, you can have multiple applications appear on a split-screen. You can also change the size of the windows of each application.

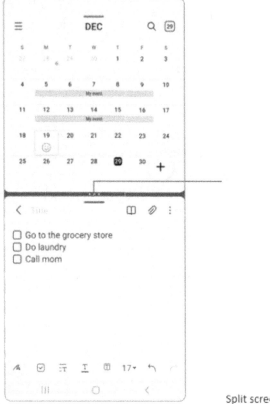

Split screen control

Split screen control

To start a split screen control session, tap the Recent apps icon from your device's home screen. Then tap on an app from the other window to bring it to the split screen. You can also drag the middle section of the window to change its size.

The illustrations presented here are for reference only. The software and devices are constantly evolving.

Window controls

The window controls can modify the way applications appear on a split screen. Drag the middle portion of the window to change its size. You can also tap on the middle border to switch between the two windows. You can add a shortcut for an app to the Edge screen's Apps panel.

Edge panels

The Edge panels, which are customizable, let you access various applications, contacts, and tasks from the edge. They can also be used to view sports, news, and other information.

To enable this feature, go to your device's settings and select Edge panels.

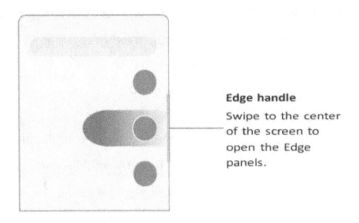

Edge handle
Swipe to the center of the screen to open the Edge panels.

Apps panel

To enable this feature, go to your device's settings and select Edge panels. You can also add applications to the Apps panel.

Drag the Edge handle over the center of the screen and swipe until the ⋮⋮ Apps panel appears.

To open an app or a pair of apps, tap on the respective shortcut. You can also tap on the complete list of applications.

To open multiple windows in a pop-up view, go to the Apps panel and drag the icon.

These illustrations are only for reference purposes and do not reflect the current state of the software and devices.

To configure Apps panel:

Drag the Edge handle over the center of the screen, and swipe until the Apps panel appears.

To add more applications to the Apps panel, tap Edit.

To add an app to the panel, go to the left-hand side of the screen and locate it. Then tap on it to add it to the right column.

Drag one application from the left-hand screen over another in the right-hand column to create a shortcut for folders.

Drag an app to the desired location in the panel and change the order of the applications. You can also remove an app by pressing the "Remove" button.

Configure Edge panels

In the settings, go to Edge panels and select the option to customize them. There are a variety of options that allow you to disable or enable each panel. You can also customize individual panels or search for those that are already installed.

Drag the panels to the right or left to rearrange their order. You can also remove them from your device and configure them with a new secure screen lock. You can also hide the panels on the lock screen when the feature is enabled.

To save changes, go to the settings and select the option to customize the Edge panels. Drag the Edge handle over the edge of the screen to change its position. You can also set which side of the panel will show in the foreground.

Lock the handle position to prevent it from being moved whenever held or touched.

The choice of a color for the Edge handle can be selected from the drop-down menu. Transparency can be adjusted by dragging the slider. The width can also be changed to fit the Edge handle. When the handle is touched, the vibrate will be turned on.

The license information and current software version of the Edge panels feature are shown in the About Edge panels section. You can also enter text messages using a keyboard or voice.

The software and devices are constantly evolving, so the illustrations presented here are only for reference.

Expand toolbar

Toolbar

The keyboard's toolbar offers quick access to the various features. Depending on the service provider, the options may vary. From the [image] keyboard, tap on the expand button to access the following options: [image] Expression: Look through a variety of emoji, GIFs, and custom emoticons. The [image] clipboard can also be used to access the various features of the keyboard, such as searching for text messages and making custom combined emojis.

Switching to a one-handed keyboard is ⚙ : enabled on the Galaxy S23 Ultra. You can also use your handwriting to type text using the device's 🖊 handwriting feature. You can also customize the keyboard by separating it into a split version.

A ⌨ ʃfloating keyboard can be used to change the appearance of the keyboard. It can be used to move it around the screen.

In the keyboard, ▢ you can search for specific phrases or words in your conversations and ▢ translate those into another language. You can also . ▢ extract text from the content of your chosen articles. You can use ⬤ Samsung Pass, which allows you to access online accounts and personal data with biometric authentication.

Grammarly provides suggestions based on your typing. You can also use emojis, animated GIF files, and emojis in stickers with the help of Bitmoji, Mojitok, and AR Emoji. You can additionally add music to Spotify through its API.

You can also add videos from YouTube using the keyboard's built-in tools. You can customize its height and width and set text editing features to help you cut, copy, paste, and highlight text.

Configure the Samsung keyboard

You can set the keyboard's type and the languages that it supports.

To switch between your preferred language and another one, tap the Space bar at the left or right.

Smart typing

Swipe the Space bar from the left or right to switch between languages. With predictive text, you can see what words and phrases are suggested based on your typing and what emojis are included when using them. You can also suggest stickers and view recommended ones while you're typing. Auto replace is a feature that replaces what you type with suggestions based on your current position.

Underline corrections are suggested for words in red and those in yellow. Text shortcuts are created for commonly used phrases. The keyboard also has more typing options and styles. The toolbar has a view or hide option.

Changing the keyboard's colors and adjusting its size can increase its overall contrast.

The keyboard can be customized with a theme or in landscape or portrait mode. Its size and transparency can be adjusted, and it can also show special characters and numbers. In addition, you can set the font size and customize the various symbol shortcuts.

There are various settings and services that are related to your voice input. You can configure the way you input gestures and feedback. You can also customize the handwriting options for the Galaxy S24 Ultra.

You can use the stylus to write in various areas of the keyboard, such as search fields and address bars. You can also convert handwritten text to PDF using the S Pen. The only model that supports this feature is the Galaxy S24 Ultra.

Save screenshots to the keyboard's clipboard and enable third-party features. You can also select the content that you want to use. To reset the default settings, go to the settings section and choose the option to revert to original.

Legal and version details for the Samsung keyboard can be found here. You can also reach out to Samsung support through its members program.

Use Samsung voice input

You can speak instead of typing with the help of the Samsung keyboard. Tap on the voice  option and speak the text that you want to enter.

Return to keyboard

CHAPTER FIVE

Camera and Gallery

The camera app allows you to take high-quality videos and photos. The Gallery app allows you to preview and enhance your captured images.

Camera

You can enjoy a variety of professional-grade features and equipment with the  camera app. To start the app, tap on the side button twice.

Navigate the camera screen

You can easily take stunning photos with your device's rear and front 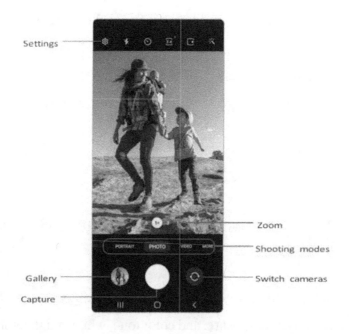 cameras. To start shooting, tap on the camera's screen and choose where you want to focus. You can also set the brightness level by dragging the slider.

You can zoom in on a specific level by tapping 1x and then selecting an option at the bottom, which is only available with the rear camera.

Settings

Zoom

Shooting modes

Switch cameras

Gallery

Capture

To change the mode for shooting, swipe the screen left or right. You can also configure the camera settings by going to the settings section and selecting Capture.

Configure shooting mode

The camera can determine the best shooting mode for your photos or choose from a variety of other shooting options.

To change the mode for shooting, swipe the screen right or left. You can also configure the camera settings by going to the settings section and selecting Capture. Portrait, Photo, and Video can be used by the camera to set the ideal settings for their respective photos.

To add more shooting options to the list, tap the Add to menu item at the bottom of the screen.

To use the Expert RAW mode, you must first download the program.

You can manually adjust the various settings, such as ISO sensitivity, exposure, and color tone, while taking photos.

In addition to ISO sensitivity, exposure, and color tone, you can also manually adjust white balance and other parameters while recording videos.

Multiple photos or video clips can be taken from different angles using the Single Take feature. You can also create a linear image by simply taking pictures in either the vertical or horizontal direction.

You can use this to take photos at night or in low-light situations without using the flash, and focus on the vibrant colors of food.

High-speed recording at a super slow-motion rate allows you to enjoy videos with exceptional detail. After you have captured a specific part of the video, it will play in slow motion.

You can create time lapse videos by recording at different frame rates. The settings can be adjusted based on the scene you're recording and the movement of your device.

For portrait videos, you can change the background of your photos.

The director's view is a feature that gives you access to a variety of advanced functions, such as lock-on and the ability to change the lens on the rear camera.

AR Zone

You can access all of your AR-related features through the AR Zone app. You can start by swiping to the left and then tap on the More button. There are a variety of features that allow you to customize your My Emoji and create a customized AR Emoji.

Enhance your videos with AR Doodle, which lets users add handwriting or line drawings to their surroundings. It also tracks the movement of objects in your environment.

Use the camera to create a Deco Pic, which allows users to decorate photos and videos in real time. It also lets users quickly measure items.

Space Zoom

The S23 Ultra's camera has a magnification of up to 100 times, which can provide you with exceptional accuracy and clarity.

To change the magnification setting, tap the Zoom shortcut from the Camera app.

When taking pictures with a higher magnification, you should place your subject in the frame and tap the Zoom lock feature to focus quickly and accurately.

Record videos

You can use your device to create smooth videos by recording in Video mode. To change the shooting mode, swipe right or left from the camera app. You can also tap the Capture option to take a picture while you're recording. To stop recording, tap the pause button.

You can enjoy immersive sound with the help of your Bluetooth headphones, which can also record 360 audio.

In the Camera app, go to the Advanced options and select the option for 360 audio recording.

Camera settings

The camera's settings can be customized through the menu and icons found on its main screen. Depending on the service provider, the options may vary.

Tap the Settings button in the Camera app. You can configure the recording method and other settings.

Intelligent features

The Scene Optimizer is a feature that will automatically adjust the colors in your photos to match the subject.

You can get on-camera help with the Shot suggestions feature, which will help you get the best possible results. You can also automatically scan QR codes for convenience.

Pictures

The shutter button is swipeable and allows users to create GIFs or burst photos.

You can add a watermark to your photos' bottom left corner. You can also choose among various file types and save options.

To save space, users can convert their photos into high-quality files. Unfortunately, some sharing platforms do not support this format.

When using the Pro mode feature, you can select the type of format that will work best for your images.

Selfies

To save photos in Pro mode, select the format that you want to use. On the other hand, you can save selfies as previews without changing their appearance.

Videos

Auto mode will automatically set the optimal frame rate for low-light conditions and produce bright videos.

To help keep the focus on the subject while the camera is moving, activate the anti-shake feature. You can also use the advanced recording options to enhance your videos.

To save space, you can record videos in the high-efficiency HEVC format. Unfortunately, some platforms and devices do not support this type of format.

Pro video recording allows users to shoot videos at a higher bitrate.

To optimize videos, you can record in the HDR10+ format. Playback devices have to support this type of video.

You can use the built-in microphone to match the zoom of the camera to the one on the other end.

You can enjoy immersive 3D sound with your Bluetooth headphones by using the 360 audio recording feature.

The camera has various features that help you ◯ capture the essence of your subject and keep it in focus. Some of these include the ability to track the movement of the subject, composing a video or picture with the help of grid lines, and attaching a GPS location tag.

Record videos

Press the volume buttons to take photos, record videos, **tap** ⦿ and control the volume of the system.

■

You can also use the ◉ camera's voice commands to take photos. For additional control, you can add a floating shutter button that can be used to take photos anywhere on the screen.

Hold your hand over the ◉ camera with your palm facing it to take a quick snapshot.

To keep the ⚙ settings relevant, you can choose whether to use the same shooting mode, mode for selfies, and filters as the previous time.

When taking a picture, the 📷 camera will automatically play a tone based on the mode selected. It can also provide vibrations when tapping on the screen.

You can view Samsung's privacy ⚙ settings and the Camera app's optional and required permissions.

You can reset the 📷 camera's ⚙ settings on your device. You can also contact Samsung through its members for assistance. You can view the app and software information of the camera.

❇ Gallery

You can view and manage all of the visual media that you have on your device by going to the Gallery.

Tap the ❇ Gallery button from the Applications section.

Customize collections of pictures and videos

You can customize the photos and videos that you've stored in the Gallery.

The images presented here are for illustrative purposes only. The software and devices are constantly evolving.

Customize collections of pictures and videos

View pictures

You can view your device's photos stored on the Gallery app. Tap the picture to view it or swipe to the right or left to view other content. You can also use Bixby Vision to take a look at the picture. Tap the Add to Favorites option to highlight the one that you want to see more.

Tap the More options to access the various features that are available to you. You can view and enhance the details of the picture, fix the image, and master it.

Drag the slider to add a portrait effect that will either enhance or reduce the background of your photos.

You can view the pictures that you have on your device using the Gallery app. To view other content, swipe to the right or left. You can also use Bixby Vision to take a look at the picture. To add a favorite image to your collection, tap the "Add to Favorites" option.

To access the various features, tap the More options. These include Details, which allows you to view and enhance the picture's information, and Remaster, which offers automatic image optimization.

Drag the slider to change the background's visibility or enhance it in your photos.

To paste the image in another app, go to the clipboard and copy the file. You can also set the picture as wallpaper, move it to a secure folder, print it, and send it to a printer. You can use the Gallery app's editing tools to enhance your photos.

To start using the Gallery app's editing tools, tap the picture you want to view and select the Edit option. You can use the Auto adjust feature to apply various adjustments to improve the image. You can also flip, crop, and twist the image to make it look different. The filters and tone feature can also change the exposure, brightness, and contrast.

Text, stickers, or hand-drawn content can be added to the picture. Revert: Undo the changes that were made to the original. When done, tap the Save option to complete the process. Play videos on your device and view the details, as well as favorites, of the ones stored.

Tap the Gallery app's pictures and videos tabs to view them. Then, tap the video to view it. Left or right swipe to view other content.

To add a video to your collection as a favorite, tap the Add to Favorites option. It will be added to the albums section under the heading "Favorites."

The More options are available to you to access the various features of the video. You can view and alter the details of the video or open it in the default player. You can also set it as a wallpaper or add it to a secure folder.

Play videos and view the content. Brightness can enhance the videos' image quality and colors for enhanced enjoyment. You can select an option from the settings. In the video editing section, tap the Edit option.

To use the various tools, tap the Edit option. Audio, volume control, and background music can be adjusted. Trim, rotate, crop, or change the overall look of the video can be done by means of transformations, filters, or other methods.

Brightness can be adjusted, contrast, exposure, and more. Effects can include text, stickers, and hand-drawn content. Revert: Undo the modifications to remove them from the original video. When prompted, confirm and then save.

To see the Gallery app's photos and videos, tap the Pictures button. You can then tap the More options to select and edit the content that you want to share.

After you've selected an app or connection to share your selection, follow the prompts to complete the process.

Delete pictures and videos

You can remove photos and videos that have been stored on your device. From the Gallery, tap the More options to select and manage the content that you want to remove. You can then confirm and delete when prompted. You can also group similar images together.

Take a screenshot

The Gallery app will automatically create a gallery of screenshots once you capture one of your screens.

To take a screenshot, press and release the Volume down and Side keys from any screen. You can then swipe to take a screenshot.

Keeping in touch with the screen, swipe across the edge to capture an image.

To enable this feature , go to the settings app's Advanced features and select the option that's related to gestures and motion capture. You can then configure the settings for screen recording and screenshots. After you capture a screenshot, a pop-up will appear with additional options that can be used to customize the content.

Sharing a screenshot using the toolbar's screenshot feature will automatically delete the saved screenshots.

Navigate bars and status bar should not be displayed on screenshots. You can choose whether to save them as PNG or JPG files. You can also choose a storage location for them.

Write notes, record your activities, and use the camera to take a video overlay to share with others.

Tap the Screen Recorder option from the Quick Settings screen.

To start recording, choose the sound setting that you want.

A three-second countdown will start recording once the gadget has started working. Tapping the "Skip" button will stop recording immediately.

When drawing on the screen, tap the Compose button. You can also show an icon for the stylus when using it with the Galaxy S23 Ultra. Tapping the Selfie video option will add a recording from your device's front camera.

To stop recording, tap the "Stop" button. These will be automatically saved to the Gallery's Screen recordings album.

Screen recorder settings

You can configure the quality and sound settings for the Screen Recorder.

Go to the settings app's Advanced features and select the option that's related to screenshots and screen recording.

The resolution of the video you want to use should be selected. You can also set the size of the overlay for Selfie videos.

Enable the option to show touches and taps in recordings. You can then save the screen recordings in a specific storage location.

The list of apps shows the list of all the pre-loaded and downloaded programs. You can also get them from the Google Play and Galaxy Store.

To access the list of apps, swipe up from the Home screen.

Go to the list of apps and choose the ones that you want to remove.

The apps that are installed on your device can be removed. On the other hand, those that are pre-loaded and labeled as disabled are hidden and can only be turned off.

Tap the "Uninstall/Disable" button from the Apps list. You can also search for specific settings or apps to find them.

Go to the search field and enter a word or phrase. As you type, the results will show up as matching programs and settings.

Go to the next app that you want to go to by tapping the result. To customize the search results, go to the Settings app and select More options. You can also sort the list of apps by category or by manually arranging them.

Empty icon spaces can be conveniently removed by pressing the More options for "Clean up pages" when the apps are organized manually.

Empty icon spaces can be conveniently removed from the list when the apps are sorted manually or through the option to clean up the pages.

Create and use folders

Folders can be made to organize the shortcuts found within the apps list.

Drag and drop one of the app shortcuts you've found on top of another one until it gets highlighted.

To create a new folder, go to the app shortcut and release it. Choose the name of the folder, change its color, and add more apps. You can also click on the "Done" button to complete the process. You can then close the folder by pressing the "Back" button.

To add a folder to the home screen, go to the Apps list, tap the Add to Home button, and then select the "Add to Home" option. When you click on the "Add to Home" button, the app shortcuts will return to the list. To remove a folder, tap the "Remove" button, and then confirm when prompted.

Game Booster

Performance boosters help you get the most out of your gaming experience by blocking notifications and enabling features that will enhance it. As you play a game, you can view the navigation bar's options by moving up from the bottom.

To prevent accidental taps, you can set the device to lock.

Performance boosters can also be configured to monitor and block various features, such as the navigation bar, screenshots, and screen touches.

You can manage the installed and pre-loaded apps through the app settings.

You can set the default apps for various activities, such as sending and receiving messages, making calls, and surfing the web.

The Samsung app settings app allows you to view and customize the various features of the company's apps.

To update or view the privacy and usage details of an app, tap it. The options for each app vary.

You can reset the settings of the app that have been changed by going to the More options and selecting the Reset preferences option.

Samsung apps

The following apps may be pre-loaded or downloaded over the air to your device. These are available in the Google Play Store and the Galaxy Store. The service provider of your network may have different options.

AR Zone

You can access all of your AR-related features through the AR Zone app. This is a convenient way to store all of your experiences.

**Bixby**

Through its customized content, Bixby learns about your interactions and suggests what you might want to consume.

For more information, refer to Bixby.

Galaxy Store

You can find and download premium apps for your Galaxy device exclusively through the Galaxy Store. You must have a Samsung account to access this feature.

Wear Galaxy Wearable

You can easily connect your Galaxy device to the Samsung Watch using the app for Android. You can also get more information about the product by visiting samsung.com.

Game Launcher

You can easily organize all of your games by using the Game Launcher app. You can also get more information about the product by visiting samsung.com/us/support.

If the Game Launcher is not featured in the list of apps, go to Settings and select Advanced features.

CHAPTER SIX

PENUP

The Galaxy S24 Ultra is a great device for sharing photos and comments on other people's creations. It also lets you browse through the pages to add something to your collection. The community features individuals who use the stylus known as the S Pen to doodle, draw, and paint.

Samsung Free

You can enjoy a wide range of content, including live TV shows, articles, and interactive games, all for free.

Samsung Global Goals

You can learn more about the campaign and contribute to its causes through the app, which has ads.

Samsung Members

Through Samsung Members, you can enjoy exclusive content and experiences only available to members, and you can get more done with your Galaxy device. You can pre-load the program on your device or download it from the Google Play or Galaxy Store.

The Samsung TV Plus

The Samsung TV Plus app is a great source of free content. It also offers a variety of other services for your mobile and TV devices.

Samsung Wallet

You can easily make payments using Samsung Wallet, which accepts almost any credit card. You must have an account with Samsung to use this feature.

Smart Switch

You can use the Smart Switch feature to transfer photos, contacts, and other content from an old device to another one.

Smart Things

The SmartThings app allows you to control and monitor various aspects of your home using a mobile device. It can be used to connect different gadgets at the same time and check their status.

The warranty of Samsung does not cover defects or errors that are not related to the company's connected devices. If you have a non-Samsung device, you should contact its manufacturer for assistance.

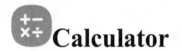# Calculator

This section offers tips and tricks, as well as a user's manual for your device. The calculator app offers scientific and basic math functions.

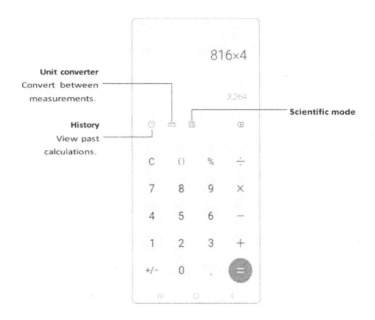

The software and devices are constantly evolving, so the illustrations presented here are only for reference.

Calendar

The Calendar app can be utilized to sync all of your appointments across multiple online accounts.

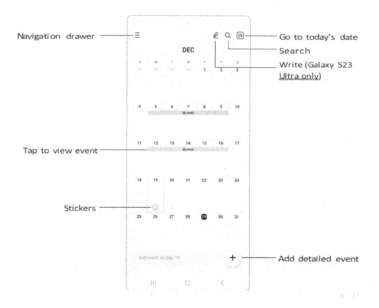

The software and devices are constantly evolving, so the illustrations presented here are only for reference.

Add calendars

You can add your contacts, email, and other accounts to the Calendar app by navigating to the navigation drawer and selecting the option to add accounts. You can also set the style of the alerts that will appear in the app for each of your contacts.

To set up an alert style, go to the 🗓Calendar app's navigation drawer and select the option "Alert style." There are three options available: light, medium, and strong. With the light option, you can receive a notification with a short sound, while the medium and strong provide a full-screen alert with ring sound until it is dismissed.

You can select the type of alert sound that you want to use based on the option you selected in the navigation drawer. For instance, you can choose the medium or light alert style. You can also customize the sound for the strong or short alert style. To create an event, tap the "Add a detail" button in the 🗓 Calendar app.

Go to the 🗓Calendar app's navigation drawer and select the option "Add a detail" button in the Calendar app. You can then click on the event that you want to remove and confirm it. You can also tap on an event to edit it. The app's features allow you to keep track of your time and set alarms.

The Calendar 📅 app's illustrations are only for reference purposes and should not be considered a comprehensive overview of the software or device.

Alarm

The Alarm tab can be used to set recurring or one-time alarms. You can also configure the alarm's schedule and choose the method for which it will be sent. To configure it, go to the ⏰ Clock section and tap on the "Add alarm" button. You can then select the day and time of the alarm's release.

Alarm in 43 minutes
Thu, Dec 29, 12:00 PM

Add alarm

Turn alarm on or off

6:00 AM   S M T W T F S

12:00 PM   S M T W T F S

5:00 PM   S M T W T F S

Alarm   World clock   Stopwatch   Timer

You can select the sound that you want to play for the alarm and set the volume of it.

Vibration can be selected to set the alarm's frequency and duration. Snooze can be enabled to set intervals and repeat values while you're sleeping. You can then save the alarm by pressing the "Save" button.

You can add ✛ a bedtime reminder and automatically set your device to sleep mode when it's time to fall asleep.

Delete an alarm

You can remove the alarm that you made by pressing the "From Clock 🔘" and holding it. You can also do this by going to the Alert settings and selecting the option "Delete."

The device can vibrate for timers and 🔘 alarms if the mode for sound is mute or vibrated.

Go to the Settings app and select the "Alarm" option. You can set the frequency and duration of the alarm and enable the feature to set a silent mode when the system sounds is off. You can additionally receive notifications about upcoming alarms by pressing the notification button.

The world clock

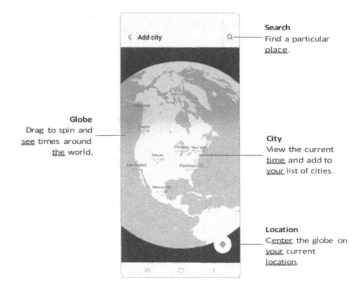

Search
Find a particular place.

Globe
Drag to spin and see times around the world.

City
View the current time, and add to your list of cities.

Location
Center the globe on your current location.

The world clock allows you to keep track of the time in various cities across the globe. You can also add a city by dragging it to the globe, selecting its name, and then pressing "Add." You can then choose to remove it by holding it or touching it.

All of the illustrations presented are for reference only and should not be considered an exhaustive overview of the device or the software.

Time zone converter

You can also set a time in a city on your world clock to view the local time in the other cities.

From Clock, tap the world clock. You can also go to the options section and select the time zone converter. You can then choose a different city by pressing the "Add" button.

To set a time, swipe the time, hours, and minutes on the clock face. The time for the other cities will automatically update.

Weather settings

To return the clock back to the current time, tap the Reset button. You can enable or disable the display of weather information by going to the settings section and selecting the "Show weather" option. You can also tap the temperature to change it from Fahrenheit to Celsius. Finally, you can select the Stopwatch feature, which allows you to time events by a hundredths of a second.

To stop the clock, tap the Stopwatch option from the clock face. You can then start timing and track the laps that you have completed by pressing the Lap Switch. To stop the clock, tap the Stop to end timing. You can then reset the feature by pressing the Reset button. You can set a countdown timer for 99 hours, 59 minutes, or 59 seconds.

To set the time, tap the "Timer" button from the Clock app. You can also use the keypad to set the parameters of the device such as the hours, minutes, and seconds. To stop the timer, tap the pause button. Tapping the "Resume" option will allow you to continue working with the feature. You can then set the name and save the preset timers in the app.

Go to the settings section and select the "Add" button to save the timer. You can also customize the appearance of the timer by going to the "More options" section and selecting the "Edit" button. You can additionally choose the sound that you want to use.

You can set the timer to vibrate and show a pop-up window when the app is minimized. You can also customize its appearance by going to the settings section. In the next section, you can look through the various settings for the Clock app.

You can easily customize the content of your apps through the Sign in feature of your Samsung account.

CHAPTER SEVEN

Contacts

You may contact Samsung through its members. You can also check the current version of the Clock app and look for updates.

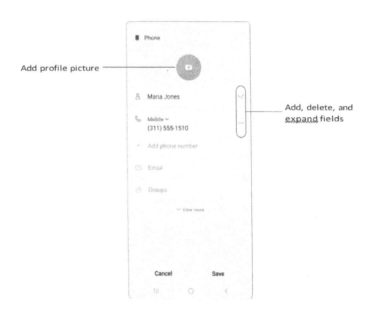

Your contacts can be stored and managed through a variety of accounts. You can also sync with other devices and use features such as email and calendars.

The illustrations presented here are for reference only and should not be considered indicative of the current state of the technology.

Create a contact

To create a contact, go to Contacts and select the "Create contact" option. Then, enter the details of the contact and select the "Save" button.

Edit a contact

You can change or remove information in a contact by pressing the field or adding more details to it.

Go to Contacts and tap on a contact. You can then go to the Edit, Save, and Delete fields to add or remove information, or change the status of the contact.

Favorites

When you select contacts as favorites, they will be grouped at the top of your list and can be easily accessed by other applications.

From Contacts is a simple way to organize and manage your contacts. You can also tap on a contact and select the "favorites" option to mark it as a favorite. You can then share it with others using various sharing methods. You can also tap either the Text or vCard files to save and manage the contact.

When viewing a contact, tap the More > QR code to share the contact information with your friends and family. The code will update automatically whenever you change the fields.

Show contacts when sharing content

You can share content with your contacts in various applications by enabling the feature. The Share window will show your frequent contacts.

Groups

You can group your contacts to organize them. To create a group, go to Contacts and tap on the navigation menu that's labeled "Groups." You can then enter the details of the group and its name. You can also customize the group's ringtone.

To add a new contact to a group, go to Contacts and select the "Add member" option. You can then save the contact and add or remove it from the group. From Contacts, tap the Show navigation menu and select groups. You can also hold and touch a contact to select it or remove it.

Go to the Edit, Add member, and select the contacts that you wish to add. You can then save the contact once you're done.

Send a message to a group

You can also send a message to a group using the group option from Contacts. You can then tap on the navigation menu that's labeled "Groups" and select the groups that you want to add. You can then send an email to the group using the group option.

Go to Contacts and select the contacts that you want to add. You can then tap the All option at the top of the list to select all of them.

Only those members of the group who have an email address are shown.

Delete a group

You can easily remove the group and its members by dragging them to the trash. You can also export or import contacts and link multiple entries into one contact list.

Merge contacts

By linking multiple entries into a contact, you can consolidate contacts information from different sources.

To manage your contacts, go to the navigation menu and select the Manage contacts option.

To merge multiple contacts, go to the Contacts menu and select the "Merge contacts" option. You can then view and organize the list of contacts that have multiple phone numbers, addresses, and names.

Import contacts

Follow the prompts to import contacts.

You can import contacts into your device using a vCard file. Go to Contacts and tap on the navigation menu that's labeled "manage contacts." Follow the prompts to complete the process.

Export contacts

You can export contacts to a vCard format from your device.

Navigate to the Contacts app and tap the Show navigation menu for managing contacts. Then, follow the prompts to export contacts.

You can export contacts to a vCard format from your device.

Navigate to the Contacts app and tap the navigation menu for managing contacts. You can then follow the prompts to export contacts.

Keep all of your contacts synchronized in all of your accounts. You can manage your contacts from the Contacts app's navigation menu. You can also delete multiple contacts at once. To select a contact, tap and hold it. You can then tap on other contacts to remove them as well.

In the settings, select Safety and emergency, and then choose Emergency contacts. You can call these contacts even while your device is locked. To add a member, go to the Safety and emergency category, and choose your preferred contacts. You can also show and hide emergency contacts on the lock screen to allow quick access to them in case of an emergency.

Samsung Internet

The Samsung Internet is a fast and reliable web browser that's designed to give you a better browsing experience. It also comes with a variety of security features to protect your privacy and speed up your online surfing.

To learn more about the Samsung Internet, please visit the company's website at samsung.com.

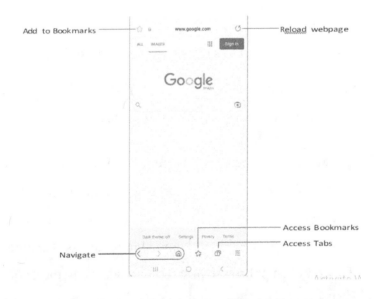

Due to the constantly changing nature of software and devices, the illustrations presented here are only for reference.

Browser tabs

A browser tabs allows you to view multiple webpages at once. You can also create a bookmark to keep track of your favorite sites and open them later. From the Internet, go to the Tabs > New tab and select the Add to bookmarks option.

In the Internet app, go to the Bookmarks section and tap the Add a page option. There are also various other ways to save a page. You can add a page to your bookmark list, view a list of saved pages, or manage other commonly visited websites.

To shortcut a particular page, go to the Home screen and create a shortcut for it. You can also use the saved pages feature to access the content of the site on your device so you can access it without being able to access it online. To view a list or browse past recent visits, go to the Tools > History section and tap the More options option.

You can easily share web pages with your contacts by going to the Tools > Share option and following the prompts.

In Secret mode, webpages are not displayed in your device's search or browser history, and no traces of cookies or other data are stored on your gadget.

After you close the secret tab, any files that you have downloaded remain on your device.

You can keep downloaded files on your device after closing the secret tab. To switch to the secret mode, go to the Tabs app and turn on its feature. You can also set up a biometric lock or password to use it. To enable the mode, go to the More options section and select the option to create a password.

To remove all traces of your secret mode data, go to the Reset option and then restore your defaults. Turn off the secret mode and enable it again. You can also go to the Internet settings and modify the settings that are associated with the app that you use to access the web.

The Messages app lets you send emojis, share photos, and make quick hellos to your contacts. The options offered by different service providers may vary.

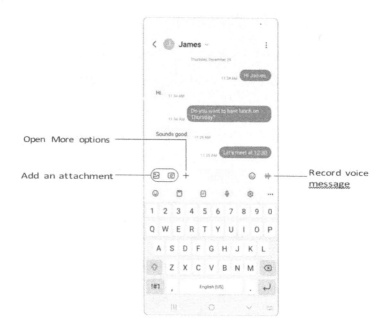

Message search

The message search feature is useful if you're looking for a message. You can start by going to the 💬 Messages app's search field and entering keywords.

The illustrations presented here are for reference purposes only. The devices and software used are constantly evolving.

Delete conversations

You can remove the conversion history of your contacts by deleting all of their conversations. To do so, go to the Messages app's More options and select the option to Delete all of your conversations. You can also send a message with audio and pictures to your contacts as an emergency.

Go to the Settings app and select Emergency SOS. You can start the following steps by pressing the Side key multiple times.

Before you start implementing emergency actions, set the countdown to one second. You can also make an emergency call and set the number to which you want to dial. You can also enable sending your location to your contacts.

Volume down and side keys can be used to activate Emergency SOS. Tapping on the emergency call will activate this feature.

Emergency sharing

You can send audio and pictures to your contacts in case of an ⚠ emergency.

To customize the notifications that you receive for emergency calls, go to the Safety and emergency section of the Settings app.

You can access ⚠ emergency notifications through the Settings app. To access the Advanced settings, go to the Notifications section and select Wireless Emergency Alerts.

My Files

You can view and manage all of the files that you have on your device, as well as those that are stored in your cloud accounts.

The software and devices used are constantly changing, so the illustrations presented here are only for reference purposes.

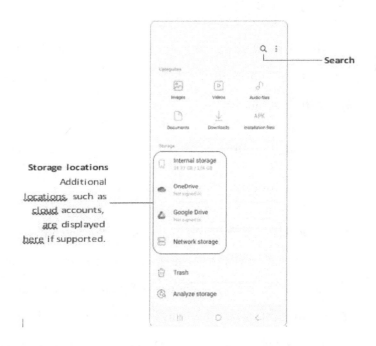

Search

Storage locations
Additional
locations such as
cloud accounts,
are displayed
here if supported.

File groups

The files that are stored on your device are sorted into the following groups. The Recent ones show the most recent ones, while the categories allow you to view your files based on their type. You can also see all of your saved files in the cloud accounts.

My Files settings

The different cloud accounts that you use are based on the services that you sign up for. You can also check the space that's being used up.

Your service provider's options may vary, so utilize My Files' settings to configure your own options.

To navigate to the settings page, go to the My Files app and select the option that you want to configure. You can also manage the various features of your cloud accounts. You can customize the way files are displayed and deleted, as well as the access to mobile data. You can also set the file size that you want to flag when analyzing the storage.

CHAPTER EIGHT

Phone

The Phone app offers a variety of advanced calling capabilities. You can request additional information about these features from your service provider. The app's appearance and the available options vary depending on the network provider.

The illustrations presented here are only for reference purposes. The devices and software used are constantly changing.

The Phone app lets you answer or make calls from the home screen or the Recents or Contacts tabs.

You can make and answer calls from the home screen or the Recents or Contacts tabs. To make a call, go to the Phone app and tap on the number that you want to use. You can also tap on the Keypad if it's not displayed. You can view the details of all of your recent calls by going to the Recents section.

Go to Contacts and tap on the contact you want to make. Then tap the call button from the Contacts app. You can also swipe across the contact to answer it.

The name or phone number of the person calling is displayed as the phone rings. The incoming call appears as a pop-up window if you're using an app.

The details of the call, including the name and phone number of the individual calling, are displayed when the call is received. A pop-up window for the incoming call appears if you're a user of an app.

Drag the option to the right to answer or decline the call. Alternatively, you can tap the option to answer the call and decline it.

Decline a call

Decline an incoming call and a pop-up window will appear for the call if you are a user of an app.

Drag the option to decline the call and forward it to voicemail.

To reject the call and forward it to voicemail, tap the Decline option on the incoming pop-up screen.

Decline with a message

You can listen to the person calling using either the speaker or a ⚇ Bluetooth headset.

You can adjust the volume or switch to a speaker or headset while you're on the phone. You can also multitask while you're on the call. You can listen to the call through either a Bluetooth 🔊 headset or a speaker.

Multitask

If you're not using an app and want to switch to another one, the status bar will show the active call. To return to the contact list, tap on the notification panel and scroll down to the notification section. You can also end a call by dragging the status bar down to the 📞 end of the call.

You can choose a video or picture to show when receiving or making a call. 📞 You can also set the layout and type of background for the call. For instance, you can show the caller's information when their profile picture is displayed.

Calls made while using other apps may be displayed as previews.

To set the display of calls while using apps, go to Settings > Call display. There are several options that you can choose from.

The Phone app can show an incoming call on its full screen. On the other hand, it can show a small pop-up window at the top. You can also enable the option to keep the calls in this pop-up window after they have been answered.

You can manage your calls by keeping track of their details in a call log, which includes the speed dials, voicemail, and block numbers that you have set up. The log also holds the numbers of calls that you have received, missed, or dialed.

Tap the Recents option from the Phone app to see a list of calls made recently. The name of the individual calling is shown if they are in your Contacts list.

Save a contact from a recent call

You can use recent call details to add or update contacts in your Contacts list. To do so, go to the Recents option from the Phone app.

To save the call's details to your Contacts list, tap on it and select Add contacts.

Go to the call and select the information you want to save. Then, tap the Add contacts option.

Go to the contact list and select Update or Create new contact. You can also delete call records by pressing and holding the phone and then tap the Delete button. You can then block a number by pressing and holding the phone.

Block a number

Placing a call from this number into your block list will result in it being forwarded to your voicemail and no messages being received.

To add a contact to the ⊘ block list, go to Recents, select the caller, and then select ⓘ Details. You can also block or update the contact by pressing the Block option, and then confirm it when prompted.

In the settings, you can modify your block list. You can also tap on the option to block numbers from the Phone app.

Speed dial

A shortcut number can be assigned to a contact so that they can speed up their dialing. You can access the details about the reserved speed numbers through the options in the options section of the Phone app.

Unassigned numbers can be selected by going to the menu and choosing a different speed ⓒ dial number than the one that's in sequence. For instance, Number 1 is for Voicemail. You can also type in a name for the number or add it to the Contacts list to assign it to the contact. The selected number will be displayed in the box that's for the selected contact.

Dial the speed dial to make a call. C You can do this by holding the number and touching it from the Phone app.

First, enter the first few digits of the speed dial number, and then hold the last one.

Remove a Speed dial number

You can remove an assigned speed dial number. Go to the Phone app's settings and select More options for speed dial numbers. Then, tap Delete the contact you want to take away from the list.

Emergency calls

Regardless of the service status of your phone, you can still C call the emergency number in your region. You only have to make an emergency call if the phone is not activated.

Go to the emergency number that you want to call and click on the Call button. You'll be able to access various in-call features during this type of call.

Even if your phone is locked, you can still use it to make an emergency call. The only person who can access this feature is the one who needs help. The rest of the device is secure.

Phone settings

You can modify the settings for the Phone app through the options in its settings. Some providers support different calling services. You can also place multi-party calls and make another call while others are still on the line.

Depending on the service provider, the options may vary. To add a call to another number, go to the active call and tap the Add call button. Once the call is answered, switch the numbers and hear the two callers at the same time. You can also make a video call using the Phone app, enter the number and then tap the Meet or Video call option.

Some devices do not support video calling. If the receiver accepts the video call, they can also use a regular voice call to answer it.

Video call effects

You can also customize the background of a video call in the apps that support it. In the settings section, go to the Advanced features and select Video call effects. You can then enable this feature.

You can automatically change the virtual background color to a solid color depending on your surroundings using this feature.

You can also choose the image from your photos that you want to use as the video backdrop.

Wi-Fi calling

You can make calls over the Internet using the phone when you're connected to a public Wi-Fi network, as long as you have the necessary settings enabled. After you've enabled this feature, follow the steps to configure it and set it up. You can also use Real Time Text to send and receive text messages while you're on the call.

Real Time Text (RTT)

RTT works seamlessly when calling an individual who has a compatible RTT-enabled phone or a teletypewriter device. Upon receiving an incoming call, the RTT icon appears.

From the Phone app, go to the settings section, and then choose Real Time Text. You can also set the visibility of the RTT call button. It can be shown only during calls or on the keypad.

You can hide the RTT keyboard when connected to an external TTY keyboard or select the preferred TTY mode.

You can easily track your daily life activities through the Samsung Health app, which provides a variety of tools and services to help improve well-being.

The data collected by this app and its associated software are not intended for the diagnosis, mitigation, treatment, or prevention of any disease.

The data collected by the app and its related software may be affected by various factors such as the environment, your device's settings, and the activities that you perform while wearing or using it.

Before you start exercising

Although the app is helpful in tracking your activity, it's still important to consult with a doctor before starting a new exercise program. Experts say that even though moderate exercise is generally safe for most people, it's important to talk to a healthcare provider before starting a new exercise regime.

The app may collect data related to various health conditions, such as diabetes, heart disease, lung disease, or kidney disease Arthritis.

Before you start an exercise program, make sure that you consult a doctor if you have any symptoms that are suggestive of a serious illness.

Some of the common symptoms of a serious illness include: pain in the chest, neck, or arms, loss of consciousness, and a feeling of dizziness. Other conditions such as ankle swelling and a heart rhythm issue may also occur.

You should also consult a medical professional before exercising, especially if you have a variety of health issues or are pregnant. Discuss this with your doctor if you are not sure about your condition.

Samsung Notes

With Samsung Notes, you can easily create and share notes that include text, music, and images. You can also use social networking services to share them.

You can also find more information about the Samsung Notes app and its features by visiting the company's website at samsung.com.

Although the images presented here are for illustrative purposes only, the products and software used are constantly evolving.

Create notes

You can easily add photos, text, and voice recordings using the Add option from Samsung Notes.

Voice recordings

An annotated voice recording is ideal for meetings or lectures, and it can be taken notes while you're recording audio. Playback allows you to scroll through the text.

To add content while the audio is being recorded, tap the Add option from the Notes app. You can also use the text option to create content while the audio is being worked on. You can also make changes to the notes that you've created. To navigate to the next section, tap the "view" button and select "Edit."

You can import PDF files in Samsung Notes. You can also search for a keyword. There are also more options when it comes to editing notes, including the ability to share, move, lock, or save as a file. You can also switch between the Simple, List, or Grid categories. Keep your notes at the top of the page with the Pin favorites option.

The navigation menu in the Notes app displays the notes by category. You can also view all of your notes by choosing the option to view all of them. You can also view shared notebooks, which are linked to your contacts through the Samsung account, as well as trash, which is a collection of deleted notes that you can view for up to 15 days.

 **Drive**

You can easily browse the Internet using Chrome, and bring your address bar, open tabs, and bookmarks from your desktop to your mobile device.

 **Gmail**

You can access, view, and share files stored in your Google Drive cloud account through the Drive app. You can also send and receive emails with the web-based Gmail service.

Google

With tools that let you identify what interests you, you can find the content that you want. Turning on your personalized feed will let you receive content that is customized.

To learn more about Google's web search capabilities, please visit the company's support page.

Google TV

You can also find more information about Google's search capabilities by visiting support.google.com. Google TV is a streaming media player that lets you watch movies and TV shows that have been purchased from the Google Play store.

Google Maps.

You must enable location-based services in order to use Google Maps.

To learn more about Google's mapping capabilities, please visit support.google.com.

Meet

Google Maps is compatible with a wide range of devices, including smart phones, tablets, and the web. You can make and receive video calls across different platforms, and you can sign up for messaging using the official app of Google.

Google Photos

You can store and backup your photos and videos in the Google Photos app and automatically send them to your Google account.

Play Store

The Play Store offers a variety of different types of media and apps, including movies, TV shows, books, music, and games.

▶ YouTube Music

You can use Google Wallet to pay for apps and stores using your Android phone. You can also watch and upload videos on YouTube right from your device. YouTube Music lets you stream and browse the music and albums that are featured on its platform.

The following Microsoft apps can be pre-loaded on your device. You can find them on the Google Play store or the Galaxy Store.

Outlook

You can use Outlook to manage various tasks and email, as well as access your contacts and calendar. You can also add an account to the platform by visiting support.office.com.

The images presented are for illustrative purposes only and do not reflect the current state of the art of software and devices.

Send message

Show formatting options

Add attachment

 Microsoft 365

You can use the Microsoft 365 app on your device to view and manage various professional files, such as Word, Excel, or PowerPoint.

OneDrive

You can easily store and share photos, documents, and videos in your OneDrive account, which can be accessed from any of your devices.

Access Settings

You can access your device's settings ⚙ by going to the Home screen, choosing the Apps, and then selecting the Settings ⚙ option. If you're not sure where to go to find the specific setting that you want, you can use the search 🔍 box to look for it.

Go to the Connections 📶 section and select the option that you want to manage your device's connections.

CHAPTER NINE

Wi-Fi

Without using your mobile data, you can access the Internet using a Wi-Fi network.

Tap the Connections icon and choose the Wi-Fi option. You can then turn on and scan for the available networks.

After you've selected the network that you want to connect to, enter your password. You can then tap the "Connect" option to connect to a hidden network.

Connect to a hidden Wi-Fi network

If the network that you want to connect to is not listed after the scan, you can still use this method manually. Before you start, make sure that you have the necessary details, such as the password and name of the network administrator.

Go to the Connections section and select the option that you want to connect to. You can then enter the details about the network that you want to connect to. You can also select a security option and enter the password.

The network password must be entered. You can then select the hidden network option and configure other features, such as proxy and IP.

Scan the QR code using your device's camera to access the Internet.

Wi-Fi Direct

Wi-Fi Direct is a feature that allows devices to share data using the Internet. After turning on Wi-Fi, follow the steps in the next section to connect to the app and disconnect from it.

From the Connections section, navigate to Wi-Fi Direct and select More options. Then, tap the device that you want to disconnect from it.

Intelligent Wi-Fi settings

You can customize the type of networks and hotspots that you can connect to, as well as manage your saved networks. The options offered by service providers may vary.

Go to the Connections section and select the option that you want to turn on Wi-Fi. Then, go to the More options section and select the option that you want to use for intelligent Wi-Fi.

When enabled, you may choose to use mobile data whenever the connection on your device is unstable. The signal strength of the Wi-Fi helps you switch back to the Internet.

You can automatically choose to use faster and more stable Wi-Fi networks by turning on Wi-Fi in designated areas.

The Wi-Fi network quality information that you're looking for will be displayed in the list of available networks.

Priority should be given to real-time data, as well as video calls and games that are sensitive to lag.

You can also receive notifications when there are suspicious activities detected on your current network.

There are also various power saving modes that can help reduce your device's battery usage. One of these is Auto Hotspot, which automatically connects to a Wi-Fi hotspot whenever it's detected.

Various options are available to configure your device's connectivity to different types of hotspots and networks, as well as manage your saved networks.

Go to the Connections section and select the option that you want to turn on Wi-Fi. Then, go to the More options section and select the option that you want to use for advanced settings. You can also sync your Samsung account's Wi-Fi profiles. When you open an app, you'll be notified that there's a Wi-Fi network available.

Wi-Fi and network notifications let you know when there are open networks nearby.

You can view and configure your saved networks and determine whether to automatically reconnect or disconnect from specific networks.

The history of your Wi-Fi usage shows the apps that have turned it on or off recently. You can also view the status of your network and connect to the latest hotspots with the help of Hotspot 2.0, which supports automatic connectivity.

Bluetooth

You can pair your Bluetooth-enabled device with other Bluetooth-enabled gadgets, such as Bluetooth headphones and car audio systems. When a pairing is made, the two devices will remember each other and be able to exchange data without needing to enter the password again.

To turn on ⬤ Bluetooth, go to the settings app and select Connections. 📶 Follow the prompts to connect and use the feature when sharing a file. You can also rename a paired device. Doing so will make it easier to identify the device.

Go to the Settings ⚙ section and select the option to change the name of the device. Then, enter the new name and tap "Rename." You ⬤ can unpair the Bluetooth device.

Unpairing from a Bluetooth device causes it to no longer recognize the other device, which means you will have to pair it again to connect.

Go to the settings app and select the Connections 📶 option. Then, turn on Bluetooth and select the option to enable advanced settings ⚙. You can confirm the pairing by pressing the unpair button.

Advanced Bluetooth settings

The Advanced menu offers additional Bluetooth capabilities, though your service provider may have different options.

Tap the Connections option from the Settings app . You can then select the More options section to configure your device's advanced settings.

You can sync files using your Samsung account and enjoy music streaming through your Bluetooth speakers or headphones.

You can sync your device's music and settings to use it whenever you receive calls from a Bluetooth device. You can also check the status of your Bluetooth usage and view the apps that have been using Bluetooth recently.

The Bluetooth scan history shows the apps that have been detected for your Bluetooth devices and lets you manage the connectivity features of those apps.

Dual audio

You can enjoy audio from one Bluetooth device to another through dual audio. To do so, connect your Bluetooth audio gadgets to your device and then from the Notification panel, choose Media output. You can then play audio from the two devices by selecting the option next to them.

NFC and payment

Through Near Field Communication, you can make payments and send and receive payments without a network connection. Some payment apps and Android devices support this technology. Before you can start using it, you must have a device that supports NFC, and it should be within four centimeters from your Bluetooth device.

Tap the Connections option from the Settings app and select the option to enable Near Field Communication and Contactless payments.

Tap and pay

An NFC payment app can be used to make payments by simply touching your device to an authorized credit card reader. You can turn on NFC from the Connections option in the Settings app. On the other hand, you can tap Contactless payments to view the default option. You can also choose from an available payment app.

To use an open payment app, tap the "Pay" button and choose the option to use it. To set a default payment service, tap "Others." You can also enable the ability to identify the exact location of nearby devices through ultra-wideband. To access this feature, go to the Settings app and select the "Connections" option.

Airplane mode

When in airplane mode, your device will stop supporting various network connections, such as mobile data, calling, and Wi-Fi. While this mode is enabled, you can still turn on Bluetooth and Wi-Fi in the Quick settings panel or the Settings app.

To enable Airplane mode, go to the Connections option and select the option for Airplane mode.

The use of mobile devices on ships and aircraft may be subject to local and federal regulations. In addition, using ultra-wideband technology on a ship or aircraft is prohibited, and Airplane mode will disable it. Follow the crew's instructions and check with the appropriate authorities before using your device.

SIM manager

Some wireless service providers allow customers to use a dual SIM card or an eSIM for managing their multiple mobile accounts. The options for this feature may vary depending on the service provider.

Dual SIM-equipped devices have two SIM card slots, and they can also support expandable storage. These types of devices will receive software updates after they're released, which adds the capability to use dual SIM.

Devices that support e-SIM can be programmed so that they can work independently of a physical SIM card. This enables the ⬤ former to be used for data and voice calls. 📶 After they're released, these will get software updates that will allow them to have built-in e-SIM capabilities.

From the Settings app, go to the SIM manager and select the option to view and disable your physical SIM cards. You can also add eSIMs ➕ to different plans or change the settings of an old device.

When using several SIM cards, you must set a primary card for data, texts, and calls.

In the Manage your SIM cards section, you can explore the various options for your cards.

Mobile networks

You can configure your device's capability to access mobile networks and send and receive mobile data. The choices made by your service provider may differ.

Tap the Connections option from the Settings app and select the mobile networks section.

Mobile data is a feature that enables your device to send and receive mobile data.

You can configure the international roaming settings for texts, voice, and data.

You can configure the type of access that you can make to the networks while roaming. You can also enable data usage while traveling across different networks.

You can also enable the use of LTE data to enhance the communication experience. If your service provider provides this option, you can select the CDMA roaming mode.

The Access Point Names option allows you to add or choose the network settings that your device needs to access.

Choose the preferred or available networks depending on your device. You can also collect information about your device's usage and diagnostic history to help with troubleshooting.

Wi-Fi and mobile data limits can be customized. You can also check your current consumption by going to the Connections option and selecting the Data usage option.

Turn on Data saver

To conserve your data usage, turn on Data saver. It will prevent apps from accessing data in the background.

Tap the Data saver option from the Connections menu.

Go to the Data saver option and turn it on. It will prevent apps from accessing the data in the background.

To enable certain apps to use data without restrictions, select the option to allow it while Data saver is turned on. Then, tap on the respective app to specify the restrictions.

Monitor mobile data

You can configure the networks and data limits for Wi-Fi to ensure that you have the best possible experience when using the internet.

You can monitor data usage by app or view it in total.

Mobile hotspot

The Mobile hotspot app uses your data plan to establish a Wi-Fi network for other devices. From the Settings app, go to the Connections section, then select the Mobile hotspot option.

After you have activated Wi-Fi, select your device's Mobile hotspot and enter the password to connect.

The category of connected devices is indicated under this section.

Instead of entering a password, you can use a QR code to access the Mobile hotspot for other devices by scanning it.

Configure mobile hotspot settings

You can modify the connection and security parameters of your mobile hotspot. From the Connections menu, you can select the Mobile hotspot option and view and change the network name.

You can change or view the password for the security level that you want to use. You can also choose the Band option for the Mobile hotspot. You can configure additional settings for it. One of these is the Auto Hotspot feature, which allows you to share your connection with other devices that are linked to your Samsung account.

Tethering

Tethering allows you to share your device's connection with another gadget. The options for this are dependent on the service provider.

In the Connections menu, go to the Mobile hotspot and tethering options, then select Bluetooth. You can also use Bluetooth to share the Internet connection of your device. You can connect a computer to the device through a USB cable, and tap ☐Ethernet to use the Internet connection.

Nearby device scanning

You can easily set up a connection to other devices by turning on Nearby. This feature will notify you whenever there are devices that you can connect☐ to.

Go to the Connections menu, select the More option, and then turn ☐on the Nearby feature. You can then connect to a printer.

Connect to a printer

You can easily print photos and documents from your device using a printer that is connected to the same Wi-FI network.

To configure the device, go to the settings☐ page and select the More option. Then, select the Add printer option.

If you're not sure about the type of plugin that you need, follow the steps below to install and configure it.

Some apps do not support printing.

Virtual Private Networks

A VPN is a type of secure network that you can use from your device. The information that you provide to your VPN administrator will be used to connect to the network.

Go to the settings page, and then select the More option for VPN. In the next section, you can add a VPN profile.

Tap the "Save" button and enter the details that the network administrator has provided.

Manage a VPN

VPN settings can be used to change or delete the connection. From the Connections menu, you can select the More option and then click on the VPN. You can also change or remove the VPN by going to the Settings next to it and selecting the Save option or the Delete option. Setting up a VPN is easy, as it will automatically connect to and disconnect you from the network.

Go to the settings and select the More section for VPN. Then, enter your details and select the "Connect" option. You can disconnect the VPN by pressing the "Disconnect" button. You can also configure your device to use a private DNS server.

Ethernet

An Ethernet cable can be used to connect a device to a local network if the wireless network is unavailable.

Go to the settings and select the More option for Ethernet. Then, follow the steps below to configure your device's connection. You should make sure that you have an Ethernet cable adapter.

Network lock status

The network lock status of your device and whether or not it is eligible for an unlock will be shown. The options offered by service providers may vary.

From the settings, you can configure your device to maintain mobile continuity with other connected gadgets. You can also enable Quick Share, which lets anyone with a Samsung app account share files with the device.

The Galaxy Buds can be automatically switched between devices when you make a call, play media, or answer a call.

You can make and answer calls and send text messages from other devices using your Samsung Galaxy devices that are linked to your account.

You can continue using apps on other devices using your Galaxy devices that have been linked to your Samsung account.

You can also use Windows computers to access your device's messages, photos, and other important files.

You can also use the Galaxy Book's keyboard and cursor to control various features of your device.

Samsung DeX

The Samsung DeX feature allows you to connect your device to a TV or PC for optimal multitasking.

The DeX feature also allows you to connect your Galaxy device to a TV or a PC for optimal multitasking. You can use the Smart View feature to show or play videos on your TV. The Galaxy Wearable, on the other hand, lets you connect your device to a Galaxy watch and headphones.

You can use Android Auto to connect your device to compatible car displays so you can focus on driving.

CHAPTER TEN

Sounds and vibration

The sounds and vibrations that your device makes to indicate certain actions and notifications can be controlled.

Sound mode

You can configure the sound mode of your device without the volume keys by going to the settings and selecting Sounds and Vibration.

You can use the volume levels, sounds, and vibrations that you have set in your Sound preferences to receive notifications and alerts.

You can configure your device to vibrate whenever you receive a call, as well as when you ring it.

When you ring your device, it will vibrate as well. You can also set it to only vibrate for notifications or alert sounds. You can mute your device or set a time limit for it to stop making sounds.

Instead of using volume controls to change the sound mode, use the device's sound setting to do so.

Mute with gestures

Turn the device over or cover the screen to mute the sounds. From the Settings app, select Advanced features, then Mute with gestures, and enable it.

You can set the frequency and type of vibrations your device produces.

Go to the settings app and select Sounds and vibration. You can customize the frequency and type of vibrations your device produces by choosing from a variety of preset patterns. You can also configure the system vibration option to set the frequency and feedback of the vibrations.

There are various gestures that your device can use to interact with its users. These include vibrating when you hold an item on the screen or tap on navigation buttons. It also vibrates when you press the phone keypad or when you type on the keyboard with the Samsung keyboard.

Drag the sliders to configure the intensity of the vibration for notifications, touch interactions, and calls.

Volume

The volume control for various sounds and notifications is set. Go to the settings app and select Sounds and vibration. Drag the sliders to set the intensity of the vibration for different sounds.

The Volume keys can also be used to adjust the volume of your device. When you press the menu, it displays the current sound type and volume level. You can then expand the menu and change the volume of the various sound types by dragging them.

The volume controls are used for media. You can go to the settings app and select Sounds and vibration. Drag the sliders to configure the intensity of the vibration for different sounds.

Use Volume keys for media

The default action of the volume controls can be used to control the volume of the media. It should not be set to use specific sound types.

In the settings app, tap on the Sounds and vibration option and select Volume. You can then enable this feature by pressing the Use keys.

Media volume limit

The maximum volume of your device should be limited while using Bluetooth headphones or speakers.

From the settings app, select Sounds and vibration and select Volume. Then, go to the media volume limit option and enable this feature. Drag the slider to set the maximum output. You can also change the volume setting by pressing the Set volume limit PIN option.

Ringtone

The options for customizing your call ringtone may vary depending on the service provider.

Go to the settings app and select Sounds and vibration. Then, choose the type of music that you want to use as a ring tone. You can also customize the volume of the different sounds ◀)) by dragging the slider. You can additionally set a pre-defined sound for all notifications.

Drag the slider to change the volume setting for the notification sound. Then, tap on the preview to hear it.

The settings menu allows you to customize the sounds that appear in notifications for each app.

System sound

You can cust ◀)) omize the sounds of your device for certain actions, such as charging and tapping the screen. The options for this feature may vary depending on your service provider.

From the settings app go to the Sounds and vibration section and select System sound. Drag the slider for volume adjustment.

You can customize the sound theme for different actions, such as charging and touch interactions. It can also be used to change the mode of sound and customize the volume for notifications.

Different sounds are played when you interact with your device. Some of these include playing a tone when you press the screen or tap on it to make a selection, and a tone when you type on the Samsung keyboard. You can also play a sound when you connect a charger or when you unlock the device.

Dolby Atmos

You can enjoy Dolby Atmos when you're using content that's specifically designed for the feature. This only works with a headset connected.

Go to the settings app and select Sounds and vibration. There you can configure the sound quality and effects of your device.

To configure the sound quality and effects, tap on the Sounds and vibration option. You can use Dolby Atmos for various applications, such as gaming. This feature delivers a rich and uplifting audio experience.

Equalizer

You can manually change your settings or select an audio preset that's customized to a specific genre of music.

To configure the sound effect and quality, tap on the options under Sounds and vibration. You can also choose a specific music genre.

UHQ upscaler

This enables users to enhance the audio quality of videos and music files through a connected headset.

Go to the Sounds and vibration settings app and select Sound 🔊 quality and effects. UHQ can also be upgraded and configure the sound effect and quality. In the next step, you can configure the sound for each ear and customize the experience.

After you've selected the ideal sound profile, tap on the settings to customize it. You can also test your hearing to determine the best sound for your device.

Separate app sound

You can have the app play only sound on a Bluetooth headset or speaker when paired with a device. This feature can be accessed through the Audio device menu option.

Tap the Sounds 🔊 and vibration option from the settings app and select the "separate app sound" option. Then turn on the feature and configure the sound effect for each audio device. You can choose the app that you want to play its sound on and the audio device that you prefer.

Notifications

By separating notifications sent by different apps and how they are delivered, you can optimize your notifications and reduce your time spent looking for and receiving them.

App notifications

You can filter which apps send notifications to you.

Go to the settings app and select Notifications. Then choose which apps to enable notifications for.

Lock screen notifications

You can set which notifications are shown on the lock screen. From the settings app, tap on the Notifications option and enable the feature. You can also customize the appearance of the lock screen.

Hide the notifications from the Notification panel. On the other hand, show the content in the Notification panel when the screen is opened. You can also turn on the show content option and choose which notifications to display on the lock screen when the device is locked.

You can change the style of the notifications that you receive and the additional settings that are used for them. From the settings app, tap on the notification pop-up style that you want to use.

You can choose the type of edge lighting that you want to use for your notifications. You can also customize the colors of the notifications that you want to use.

You can enable or disable the ability to show notifications on the screen while it's off.

You can configure the default Samsung settings for notifications.

Do not disturb

Turning on the do not disturb mode will block the notifications and sounds while it's still on. You can also set recurring events such as meetings and sleep.

189

From the settings app, tap on the Notifications option and select the "Do not disturb" feature. You can configure the duration of the do not disturb mode and set a schedule for when it's activated and turned off.

You can create a new schedule to set the times and days when your device will be placed in Do not Disturb mode.

Allowed while in the do not disturb mode.

To prevent calls and messages from being interrupted, tap the "Do not disturb exceptions" option.

You can add apps that you want to receive notifications in Do not Disturb mode. Even if you don't allow the linked apps, the messages, calls, and conversations will still reach you.

Enable the use of vibrations and sounds for alarms and other notifications while the do not disturb mode is active.

Advanced notifications settings

You can hide notifications by viewing customization options or opting out of receiving them. You can also configure the notifications that are sent out by different services and apps. In the Advanced settings section, click on the notification icons and modify how many appear in the status bar. You can also display the battery percentage of your device.

You can view and set priority for conversations by holding and touching the notification. It can also be turned silent or alert.

You can enable the ability to set up floating notifications, which can appear in either the Smart pop-up or the Bubbles view.

Notifications can be suggested for replies and actions. This feature allows you to reply to messages and notifications with suitable suggestions.

To snooze your notifications, enable the ability to show a button.

Enable or customize the notifications you receive from various services and apps to remind you of them regularly. You can also clear the notifications to stop them from appearing.

On the left-hand side of the notification screen, you can see which apps have active badges that appear. You can determine whether or not these are for unread messages.

You can customize the notifications that you receive for emergencies. You can also set them to alert you whenever your phone is picked up.

The device can notify you whenever there's been a missed call or message by vibrating whenever you pick it up.

To enable this feature, go to the settings app and select the "Advanced features" category. Then, select the "alert when the phone is picked up" option.

You can configure the overall display of your device by setting the font size, brightness, and timeout.

Dark mode

Turn your device's dark theme on to make your eyes feel more comfortable at night. This mode darkens the notifications and white screens.

Tap the Settings app and select the "Display" category. You can configure the device's light or dark theme depending on your preference. You can also customize the settings for the dark mode by setting the time and place when it's applied.

You can configure the Dark mode to work seamlessly with your custom schedule or sunset to sunrise setting.

Screen brightness

As scheduled, turn on Dark mode for your custom schedule or Sunset to sunrise. You can adjust the brightness of your device's screen based on your preference. In the options under Brightness, drag the slider to set a specific level.

If the Adaptive Brightness feature is disabled, you can increase the brightness by pressing the extra option. This will use more battery.

The Quick settings panel can be used to change the brightness of the screen.

Motion smoothness

The Quick settings panel can also be used to adjust the brightness of the device. You can boost the screen's refresh rate to smooth scrolling and provide more realistic animations. To configure the effect, go to the Settings app and select "Motion smoothness."

Eye comfort shield

The ability to reduce eye strain and improve sleep can be helpful. You can set a schedule that will automatically turn it on and off.

To enable the feature, go to the Settings app, select the "Display" category, and then "Eye comfort shield."

You can then customize the effect by pressing the "Customize" option.

The ability to automatically adjust the color temperature of the screen based on the time of day and your usage patterns can also be helpful.

You can set a schedule for when the eye comfort shield should be turned on or off. You can also customize its opacity by dragging the slider. This feature allows users to adjust the contrast and tone of the display to make their eyes feel more comfortable.

Screen mode

The device comes with various screen mode options that can be used to customize the quality of the screen for different situations.

In the settings app, go to the Display category and select the "Screen mode" option. Drag the slider to set the white balance. You can also manually change the device's RGB values. From the Display category, go to the

"Font size and style" option and choose a different typeface.

You can choose a font from the Galaxy Store or download one from the app. You can also make all of your fonts appear with bold weight by pressing the "bold" option. You can also change the size of text by dragging the slider. To make content easier to view, the screen zoom can be adjusted to a specific level.

Screen resolution

The resolution of the device's screen can be lowered to conserve battery power or increased to enhance the image quality.

To change the resolution of the screen, go to the settings app and select "Display." Then, choose your preferred resolution.

Some applications won't support higher or lower resolution settings. When you adjust the resolution, some of them may close.

Full screen apps

The full-screen aspect ratio allows users to choose which applications they want to use.

Camera cutout

A black bar can hide the camera cutaway.

Go to the Settings app and select the "Display" category. Then, tap on the "Apps" option to enable the camera cutouts and customize them.

Screen timeout

You can set a specific amount of time that the screen will be turned off. To set this feature, go to the settings app and select "Display," then "Screen timeout."

Keep in mind that prolonged exposure to non-moving images may lead to issues such as degraded image quality and ghost-like aftereffects. Turning off the display while not in use will also help.

Accidental touch protection

To prevent the device from detecting any touch input while it's in a dark location, such as a bag or pocket, turn off the display.

Go to the settings app and choose "Display," then "Auto-Add Accidental Touch Protection. You can then show charging information.

Show charging information

The estimated battery level and how long it would take to fully charge the device will be shown whenever the display is off.

To enable or show charging information, go to the Settings app, select the "Display," and then "Show Charging Information."

Screen saver

Go to the Settings app and select "Display" and then "Auto-Add Accidental Touch Protection." You can also enable the feature by going to the "Display" category and selecting "Increase the Screen's Touch sensitivity."

The battery level and the estimated time it would take for the device to fully recharge can be displayed whenever the screen is turned off.

You can also enable and display charging information through the Settings app. A screen saver allows you to see photos or colors on the device when the display is off or while it's charging. You can choose whether to turn this feature on or off.

You can display photos in various forms, such as a photo table or a photo frame. You can also use the Screen saver to view photos from your Google account. To learn more about the feature, tap on the "Settings" app and select "Display." Lift the device to wake it up and turn on the screen saver.

Go to the Settings app and select "Advanced features" and "Motions and gestures." Then, Lift the device to enable this feature.

Double tap to turn on screen

Instead of using the Side key, double-tapping the screen will turn it on.

You can turn off the device's display by double-tapping it instead of using the Side button.

To enable this feature, go to the Settings app and select "Advanced features" and "Motions and gestures." Then, double-tapping the screen will enable this feature.

Double tap to turn off screen

Rather than using the Side button, you can turn off your device's display using the double tap method.

Go to the Settings app, scroll down to the Advanced features, and then click "Motions and gestures," and double tap to enable this feature.

Keep screen on while viewing

The front camera should be enabled to detect when you're looking at the display to turn it back on.

To enable the feature, go to the settings app and select "Advanced features" and "Motions and gestures." Then, tap on the "Keep screen on while you're watching" option.

One-handed mode

You can make the device's layout more flexible by enabling one-handed operation. To do so, go to the settings and select "One-handed mode" from the list of Advanced features. Then, tap on one of the options to enable it.

To reduce the size of the display, tap the home button twice in succession. You can also set a screen lock, which will protect your data and secure your device.

Google apps

Google apps are available for download in the Google Play store. These may be pre-loaded on your device.

Screen lock types

There are various types of screen locks that offer varying levels of security. Some of these include PIN, Swipe, Pattern, Password, and None Screen Lock.

Biometric locks can also be used to protect sensitive data and prevent unauthorized access to your device.

Set a secure screen lock

You should always use a screen lock to protect your device. Setting up and using biometric locks is required for this type of security.

Go to the Settings app and select "Lock screen" from the list of options. You can then set a screen lock that is specific to your device.

Enable the feature and set the lock screen to show notifications. There are three options that you can choose from: hiding content, showing content in the Notification panel, and showing content once the screen has been unlocked.

You can set the type of notifications that will appear on the lock screen and also show on the Always On display feature. To exit the menu, tap the Done button. You can configure the various options for the screen lock.

You can use a smart lock feature to unlock your device whenever a trusted location or other gadget is detected. You must have a screen lock enabled for this feature.

You can customize the settings for your secure lock. You need a screen lock for this feature.

You can change the appearance and the items featured on the lock screen. You can also customize the widgets that appear on the lock screen.

Hold and touch the option to enable or disable the ability to edit the items found on the lock screen.

The Always On display option is enabled, and more information about this feature can be found here.

The time when you are at home and where you are while you're roaming will be displayed on the Roaming clock.

CHAPTER ELEVEN

Find My Mobile

Through the use of a screen lock, you can protect your device against theft or loss by allowing it to be tracked and locked online. You can also have it deleted remotely. To use Find My Mobile, you must have a Samsung account and turn on the Google location service. You can download the app from the Google Play store or visit Samsung's website for more information.

Turn on Find My Mobile

Before you can use the feature, you must first turn it on and configure the options. You can access it remotely through the Samsung website at findmymobile.com.

In the Privacy and Security section, go to the "Find My Mobile" option and select "Allow this phone to be found."

To access Find My Mobile, go to the website, select the option, and then enter your Samsung account.

Enable this to allow this feature to locate the device.

Samsung may keep your password, PIN, or pattern for remote access. This feature enables users to control their device from anywhere.

You can enable the device to send its final location to the Find Mobile server whenever its battery level falls below a certain point.

Google Play Protect

Google Play can be configured to check your device and apps regularly for potential security risks.

In the settings, go to the "Security and Privacy" section, and then select "Google Play Protect." This will enable the system to check for updates automatically.

The date of the last security update and the availability of new ones can be conveniently checked.

Tap the "Security and privacy" section and then select "Updates." You can then check for the latest security patch and see if it's available.

Permission manager

Certain apps may access certain features of your device while it's running, such as the microphone, camera, and location. You can set your phone to notify you whenever this happens.

To configure which apps can access these features, go to the settings and click on the Privacy and Security section. Then, select the category that you want to be notified of.

When you allow certain apps or services to access your device's features for the first time, a dialog box will appear asking you if you want to grant this access.

Controls and alerts

Go to the settings and click on the Privacy and Security section. You can then customize the way Samsung collects and uses your data. For instance, it can show you its privacy information and provide customized recommendations and content.

You can send Samsung details about your device whenever you encounter technical issues.

Google Privacy

You can customize Google's and Android's privacy settings. From the settings, go to the Privacy and Security section, and then select the category that you want to be notified of. You can also tap on the privacy services that are available to customize them.

Samsung Pass

You can use Samsung Pass for various services with the help of your biometric data. You need to sign in to use it.

Go to the settings and click on the "Secure Folder" option. Follow the prompts to protect your content on your device.

Secure Wi-Fi

You can get additional privacy protection through secure Wi-Fi while using networks that are unsecured. You must first sign in with your Samsung account to configure and use this feature.

Private Share

Encrypted files, set expiration dates, and block recipients from resharing them. Your information is secure with blockchain technology.

Files can be privately shared, and recipients can't reshare them. Keep your information secure using blockchain technology.

Tap the Security and Privacy option and select Private share. You can then add files by following the prompts.

Samsung Blockchain Keystore

To manage your Samsung Blockchain Keystore private key, go to the settings, and then click on the "Private share" option. The options for service providers may vary. You can also follow the prompts to set up a cryptocurrency wallet.

Unidentified third-party apps may be installed from sources or apps that you have installed. To do so, go to the Settings app and select Security and Privacy.

Unidentified apps can potentially pose a threat to your device and data due to their vulnerability to security breaches.

Password for factory data reset

A password may be required to revert your device to the factory settings on a regular basis. The options of service providers may be different.

Go to the settings app and click on Security and Privacy. You can then change or set up a password.

Set up SIM card lock

A PIN can be used to prevent unauthorized access to your SIM card. The service provider's options may vary.

Follow the prompts to set up the SIM card lock and configure other security measures.

To activate the feature, tap the lock SIM card. You can then change the PIN and create a new one. You can also view your passwords by typing short characters in the fields indicated with the names of the characters.

To turn on the feature, go to the settings app and select Security and privacy. Then, make sure that the passwords are visible.

Device administration

You can grant authorized apps and security features access to your device as a device administrator. You can go to the settings app and select the "Other security" category, followed by "device admin apps." You can then turn on the option to allow device administrators on.

Credential storage

You can manage the certificates that are installed on your device to ensure that the connections are secure.

From the settings app, go to the security and privacy section, and then select the other security options.

You can view and configure the security certificates that are installed on your device. You can also view and configure the user and security certificates that are associated with your device. You can additionally download and install new certificates from the storage or device.

Reset the password and remove the contents of your device's credentials. You can also select a certificate management app for the credential contents. You can configure different security settings to protect your device.

Tap the security and privacy tab to access the other security options. Trust agents can let trusted devices perform specific actions while connected.

This option is only available when the lock screen is enabled. For more information, please refer to the instructions on how to set a screen lock.

To prevent unauthorized access to your device's features, you can pin an app on the screen.

You can configure your device to automatically download and install Samsung updates.

To ensure that your device remains secure, check for security updates.

Location

Mobile network, Wi-Fi, and GPS are utilized by location services to determine the device's current location.

To turn on and off location services, go to your device's settings and select Location. Some applications require that you turn on location services to function. You can configure the permissions for the apps that collect and use your location data. From the settings app, tap on the "app permissions" option.

Location services

The location services use your device's most recent location data to provide you with relevant search results and improve your experience when visiting certain places.

213

In the settings app, go to your location services and select the "view how location information is used" option. You can also enable other location-based tools. To add or remove locations from the list, go to the "improvement accuracy" section and select the "add or remove method".

In addition, you can enable apps and services to automatically scan for Wi-Fi networks even when the connection is turned off.

Scan for and connect to other Bluetooth-enabled devices with the help of apps even when Bluetooth is off.

Recent access

You can view the list of apps that have asked for your location. From the settings app, tap on the "Location" option, and then select "Turn on location services." You can also view the app's settings by entering an entry.

Emergency Location Service

When activated 🔲 for emergency location service, your device will send its location to designated emergency response teams whenever you contact a certain number.

To turn on or off the emergency location service, go to the settings 🔘 app and select Safety and emergency.

Accounts

You can easily access and manage your various accounts, 🔲 such as Google, Samsung, Facebook, and ➕ email.

Add an account

You can also sync and manage your various social networking, email, and video sharing accounts. 🔲 To add an account, go to the settings app and select Manage accounts. Then, follow the steps to set up the account and enter your credentials. You can then tap 🔲 on the "auto sync data" option to automatically update your accounts.

Different account types have their own unique set of features and can be customized to suit their specific needs. The available features and settings for each type can vary.

To change the settings of an account, go to your settings app and select Manage. You can also remove an individual account from your device by pressing the "Remove" button. You can then restore or backup your data and restore it to your personal account.

Samsung account

You can backup your data to your Samsung account, though the options offered by your service provider may differ.

Go to your settings app and select Account and backup. You can configure your Samsung Cloud account to back up your data and restore it. You can also enable the backup of data to your Google account.

Go to your settings app and select Account and backup. Then, under Google Drive, select Back up data.

External storage transfer

You can restore or back up your data to a device that has a USB storage drive or a Smart Switch. Alternatively, you can bring old devices' data to this method.

Go to the Settings app and select Account and backup, then external storage transfer.

Google settings

Tap the Accounts and backup option and select External storage transfer. The Google account can be customized, and the options depend on the individual account.